Creative DBT Activities for Children Using Music

By the same authors

Creative DBT Activities Using Music
Interventions for Enhancing Engagement and Effectiveness in Therapy
Deborah Spiegel with Suzanne Makary and Lauren Bonavitacola
ISBN 978 1 78775 180 4
eISBN 978 1 78775 182 8

of related interest

Music with Babies and Young Children
Activities to Encourage Bonding, Communication and Wellbeing
Jeffrey Friedberg
Illustrated by Chlöe Applin
ISBN 978 1 78592 764 5
eISBN 978 1 78450 635 3

Music Therapy Groups with Children
Activities for Groups with Particular Needs
Amelia Oldfield
Illustrated by Lily Fossett
ISBN 978 1 78775 971 8
eISBN 978 1 78775 972 5

DBT Therapeutic Activity Ideas for Working with Teens
Skills and Exercises for Working with Clients with Borderline Personality
Disorder, Depression, Anxiety, and Other Emotional Sensitivities
Carol Lozier
ISBN 978 1 78592 785 0
eISBN 978 1 78450 718 3

CREATIVE DBT ACTIVITIES FOR CHILDREN USING MUSIC

Edited by Deborah Spiegel,
Suzanne Makary, Chelsea Steen,
and Lauren Bonavitacola

with contributions from Crystal Malinski,
Hillary Cartner-Ambrose,
Kelly Howard, and Parry Villa

FOREWORD BY ALYCIA DADD

Jessica Kingsley Publishers
London and Philadelphia

First published in Great Britain in 2026 by Jessica Kingsley Publishers
An imprint of John Murray Press

2

Mindfully Here and Now, referenced on pages 26–7 is a variation of "All I have to do is
breathe" by Patina Jackson. Find the original song on Spotify or Apple Music)
Grizzly Bear Grump song lyrics on page 111 reproduced with permission from Stephanie Leavell
Gingerbread outline on page 146 source: Shutterstock®

Front cover image source: Shutterstock®.

A CIP catalogue record for this title is available from the British Library and the Library of Congress

ISBN 978 1 80501 321 1
eISBN 978 1 80501 322 8

Printed and bound in the United States by Integrated Books International

Jessica Kingsley Publishers' policy is to use papers that are natural, renewable and recyclable
products and made from wood grown in sustainable forests. The logging and manufacturing
processes are expected to conform to the environmental regulations of the country of origin.

Jessica Kingsley Publishers
Carmelite House
50 Victoria Embankment
London EC4Y 0DZ

www.jkp.com

John Murray Press
Part of Hodder & Stoughton Ltd
An Hachette Company

The authorised representative in the EEA is Hachette Ireland, 8 Castlecourt Centre,
Dublin 15, D15 XTP3, Ireland (email: info@hbgi.ie)

Contents

Foreword

Alycia Dadd, Ph.D.

In the two decades since I began my career in school psychology, our field has witnessed an unprecedented transformation in student mental health challenges. Today's youth navigate social media anxiety, global pandemic aftermath, and escalating emotional dysregulation—phenomena that have illuminated a crucial insight: while our interventions must remain grounded in empirical research, they must also resonate with contemporary youth through modalities like music and movement that harness our intrinsic capacity for emotion regulation and self-expression.

The evolution of school psychology since the 1975 passage of Public Law 94-142 (The Education for All Handicapped Children Act/IDEA) has been remarkable. This landmark legislation mandated free and appropriate education for all students with disabilities, establishing school psychology as a distinct discipline anchored in systematic data collection and evidence-based interventions. The 1980s saw the emergence of the scientist-practitioner model in graduate programs, followed by the National Association of School Psychologists' (NASP) emphasis on preventive approaches in the 1990s—a shift that broadened school psychologists' impact on students, educators, and families.

Amid this period of professional transformation, the establishment of the Collaborative for Academic, Social, and Emotional Learning (CASEL) in the mid-1990s marked a significant development in educational psychology. CASEL's empirical research and systematic advocacy for social-emotional learning in educational settings delineated five essential competencies: self-awareness, self-management, social awareness, relationship skills, and responsible decision-making. While this framework resonated profoundly with practitioners in the field, it presented a fundamental implementation challenge: how to meaningfully integrate these competencies within the constraints of structured academic programming?

My journey with these questions began in a therapeutic support program just outside New York City, working with adolescents whose needs often mirrored those of clinical populations. As we searched for effective interventions, Dialectical Behavior Therapy (DBT) emerged as a promising approach—not only for our highest-need students but as a universal set of coping skills. Students naturally gravitated toward creative expressions of these skills, particularly through music. They would bring mindfulness activities incorporating their favorite songs, debate lyrics that captured their emotional experiences, and use music as a bridge to deeper therapeutic engagement. These moments revealed how artistic expression could transcend verbal limitations, offering alternative pathways to emotion regulation and group cohesion.

These experiences led me to Cognitive Behavioral Consultants, founded by Dr. Alec Miller and Dr. Lata McGinn, where as Director of Consultation Services I assisted with developing and implementing training programs and consultation to schools. During this time, I maintained a diverse clinical practice spanning elementary-aged students to adults, many of whom integrated artistic expression into their therapeutic work. A memorable breakthrough came during a training when a former DBT participant, now a clinician-in-training, shared an app he'd created setting DBT concepts to familiar rhythms and replacing pop song lyrics with familiar DBT acronyms. His innovative approach demonstrated how music could serve as a powerful vehicle for skill retention and emotional learning.

During this period, I collaborated with Dr. Lauren Bonavitacola, whose unique combination of clinical expertise and board certification in music therapy brought an unparalleled perspective to our clinical team. Dr. Bonavitacola consulted with several school-based teams implementing DBT and provided training on creative ways to implement skills within a group setting. Her contributions reflect both her sophisticated understanding of therapeutic principles and her exceptional ability to translate complex concepts into accessible, engaging interventions.

In my current role as Director of Mental Health in a PreK-12 school district (for children from the age of 4 through 20), I witness daily how myriad factors—the COVID-19 pandemic's aftermath, heightened concerns about school safety, intensifying academic demands, food and housing instability, and pervasive technology dependence—have significantly amplified our students' psychological needs. The combination of disrupted psycho-social developmental trajectories during periods of isolation, increased anxiety, and exposure to unprecedented levels of digital stimulation necessitates increasingly innovative approaches to therapeutic engagement and learning.

This volume presents a sophisticated synthesis of evidence-based practice and accessible clinical engagement. Deborah Spiegel, Suzanne Makary, Chelsea Steen, and Lauren Bonavitacola's approach integrates the complexity of emotional development with the inherent therapeutic power of musical expression. By combining DBT skills with musical interventions, practitioners gain a comprehensive resource that addresses both contemporary mental health challenges and music's enduring capacity for healing. As our current climate demands innovative therapeutic approaches, this integration of DBT and music provides an effective framework for engaging young clients in emotional development.

Introduction

Let us help our students:
make wise decisions,
take a step back and cool down before acting,
check the facts when making assumptions, and
regulate emotions.

The wellness of children of all ages prompted the development of this book as we, a team of therapists implementing Dialectical Behavioral Therapy (DBT) for adults and adolescents, began to adapt skills for younger and younger clientele. This shift in our clientele may be reflective of the increases of various mental health conditions that have emerged in recent years in children. From 2016 to 2020, the rate of youth diagnosed with anxiety and depression increased by 29 and 27 percent, respectively (Lebrun-Harris *et al.*, 2022). A major precipitating event that may have influenced these changes in the rates of these mental health conditions was the COVID-19 pandemic. According to the CDC, more than a third of high school students reported they experienced poor mental health during the pandemic and 44 percent reported they persistently felt sad or hopeless during the past year (Jones *et al.*, 2022). For those aged 5–11, mental health-related emergency department visits increased 24 percent from 2019 to 2020, demonstrating the increase in mental health crises children are facing (Leeb *et al.*, 2020). The full, long-term impact of the pandemic and its consequences may be yet to be seen, although what we have seen is that rates of school and mental health-related concerns have risen since the pandemic, including school absenteeism, aggressive behaviors and dysregulation in school, and social skills deficits (National Center for Education Statistics, 2022). Intervening with children in their first stages of social-emotional development, at the elementary level, may help prevent the development and/or worsening of these aforementioned psychological conditions.

Compounding this concern is the ever-increasing levels of educator and school psychologist burnout, in particular post-COVID. Educators and clinicians are being faced with the increasing demand of students' social-emotional needs, often surpassing the pace that districts can take to hire additional staff or provide other resources. The National Association of School Psychologists recommends a 1 to 500 ratio of school psychologist to student; currently NASP reports that the data from the 2022–2023 school year indicate a national ratio at 1 to 1127, with some under-resourced states as low as 1 to 19811 (2024). Therefore, the need for resources that are easy to implement, effective, and accessible to educators to increase social-emotional skills in children is clear.

In our last book, *Creative DBT Activities Using Music* (Spiegel, Makary, & Bonavitacola, 2020), we focused our musically oriented DBT interventions for an adolescent and adult audience. That book is divided into two parts. The first section has group activities for clinicians and group leaders to implement. The second section is written in a self-help format, providing music activities for teaching/reinforcing each DBT skill, which teens and adults can use themselves.

In this book, we aim to put our focus on elementary-aged children. In addition to learning an academic curriculum, we believe a well-rounded education develops the social, emotional, and cognitive growth of its pupils. According to the organization Collaborative for Academic, Social, and Emotional Learning (CASEL), 27 states have adopted K-12 social-emotional learning (SEL) competencies (CASEL, 2023). We have observed anecdotally and through emerging research how the addition of music and music therapy techniques to teach concepts such as mindfulness and emotion regulation can help engage children, facilitate learning, and create connection in creative ways (Chong, Kim, & Kim, 2024; Hwang, 2021; Moore, 2013; Moore & Hanson-Abromeit, 2015). This book design offers educators, therapists, and parents tools to enhance the social-emotional learning of children step by step with approachable and creative musical activities.

This book has derived much of its inspiration from Mazza and colleagues' (2016) book, *DBT Skills in Schools*. *DBT Skills in Schools* presents an SEL curriculum for adolescents designed to reach children at the universal level (i.e. primary prevention), not just children who are at risk or are currently suffering from severe emotion dysregulation. Students in these programs learn skills aimed at increasing emotion regulation, reducing impulsivity, and improving interpersonal effectiveness. The lessons are generally taught by general education teachers or other school personnel.

Our focus with this book is to provide lesson plans that can be easily implemented as either adjunctive (e.g. within a setting that is already incorporating DBT skills training as an SEL model) or standalone resources for educators who are interested in supplementing DBT skills training for elementary aged children with a creative and musical influence. Our aim is for these activities to engage students, teach skills, and enhance the SEL goals of the school.

The activities we have included range from one-to-one interventions to whole-classroom experiences. Some experiences may be used as a single lesson taught once, and others may be utilized on a daily basis. Attached to the lesson is a plan to implement. Also, a number of audio and/or video files are available to view at https://www.youtube.com/playlist?list=PL0jguhoPs0m 6qrlhhTR7P4PPtz7wuicy1. These are noted throughout the lesson plans and a full list of these recordings, along with a QR code to scan to access them, can be seen in the Appendix. Copies of pages marked with + can be downloaded from www.jkp.com/catalogue/book/9781805013211. Our hope has been to help guide the instructor and provide the tools to most efficiently teach the skill.

WHO ARE WE?

We are a group of DBT informed board certified music therapists who are dedicated to enhancing the lives of children through the use of music activities and songs that strengthen their social and emotional learning. In our work as music therapists, we provide a safe and engaging way for children to express their feelings, improve communication and social interaction, and build self-esteem and self-awareness. Our ultimate goal is to make a positive impact on children's lives and support their social and emotional development. We have found that by integrating DBT into our practices we can teach practical life skills that are more easily remembered and implemented into life by learning via music. This book utilizes our expertise and provides activities that an individual who has no musical know-how can easily implement. Alternatively, we do recommend hiring a DBT informed music therapist to help facilitate these and other interventions. A list of qualified DBT informed music therapists can be found at dbtmusic.com.

WHAT IS DBT?

Dialectical Behavior Therapy (DBT), created by Dr. Marsha Linehan, is an evidence-based outpatient psychotherapy model originally designed to treat extreme emotion and behavioral dysregulation in adults, that incorporates concepts from behaviorism, Eastern traditions including mindfulness, and the philosophical concept of dialectics (2015). DBT has been adapted and has demonstrated efficacy for many populations and settings over the 30+ years of its existence, including adolescents and children with emotion dysregulation (McCauley *et al.*, 2018; Mehlum, 2014; Perepletchikova *et al.*, 2017), residential treatment (Klodnick *et al.*, 2020; McCredie *et al.*, 2017), and school settings for both at-risk and universal populations (Mazza *et al.*, 2016; Zapolski *et al.*, 2022). The DBT curriculum includes a set of practical skills that teach the concepts of mindfulness, distress tolerance, emotion regulation, and interpersonal effectiveness in order to support people in replacing maladaptive behaviors with skillful behaviors, in responding to life rather than reacting, and in enhancing the lives of all.

Across the adaptations that have been made to accommodate the differing needs of various treatment populations and settings, the core DBT skills and principles have remained by and large the same. In the child and adolescent adaptations of DBT in both clinical and school settings, a main adaptation is to the language choices used to describe several skills to reflect the developmental level of a younger clientele (Mazza *et al.*, 2016; Miller, Rathus, & Linehan, 2017; Rathus & Miller, 2014). As readers explore this book, they will note this same trend of using age-appropriate language to describe some of the DBT concepts, encouraging the younger client to best understand them.

WHAT TO EXPECT

This is a collection of therapeutic music activities to teach, strengthen, and encourage the use of DBT skills with children. Our book contains music activities, songs, etc. for children ages 5–12, or people of other ages and developmental levels who could benefit from a modified and simplified version of delivery. As previously mentioned, the activities—modified to fit your age group—and skills covered could be used to supplement a DBT in Schools program and/or to develop skills outside of a structured program.

This book consists of group and individual activities for teachers, therapists, parents, and/or group leaders to use. The activities described in this book can be taught by non-musicians and musicians alike to be able to engage students with music activities and songs that help students learn, remember, and generalize the DBT skills, in a fun and creative way. They were designed by a team of board certified music therapists who completed a comprehensive DBT-Informed Music Therapy Training Program and learned the skills together through the Spiegel Academy. The activities highlight a particular DBT skill(s) along with step by step instructions for how to present the activity and skill. Included in the lesson plan are the primary aims of the lesson, materials needed, and instructions for conducting the lesson.

This book aims to provide activities that are original, as well as to showcase interventions that graduates of the DBT-Informed Music Therapy Training Program have contributed, and have graciously allowed us to include in this book. We want to thank all those who have contributed in any way to this work! Your contributions are priceless, and we are forever grateful.

The activities presented here are a mere sample of creative ways that therapeutic music interventions can be used to enhance DBT skills teaching and learning. They are meant to inspire you to generate your own ideas or to remind you of other activities you may already know that could be used to teach a DBT skill. Feel free to add, subtract, modify, improvise, or change any idea, making sure to preserve the core lessons of the DBT skill you are aiming to teach and/or strengthen.

HOW TO USE THIS BOOK

As mentioned previously, this book has aimed to design lessons that are easy to utilize with children at the elementary level. Each activity is written to the developmental level of a typical early elementary-aged child.

For each skill, there are suggested modifications listed in order to make the intervention a bit more challenging for those elementary students who are more developmentally advanced. With a diverse classroom these exercises can be modified for various levels in one room.

Although multiple skills can sometimes be highlighted through the use of one intervention, focus on one skill at a time. Stick to one core skill, starting with the skill that is listed for that specific intervention; one can repeat the lesson and change the skill focus if desired and applicable. However, our recommendation remains to focus on one targeted skill per lesson. This itself is mindfulness (the skill of "one-mindfully!"). It is also recommended that at the end of a module one reviews various skills from the entire unit using an intervention that incorporates multiple skills.

Each activity references the corresponding DBT skill it is targeting; however, it does not provide in-depth explanations of each DBT skill. For this, we recommend reviewing both the adult and adolescent DBT skills manuals (Linehan, 2015; Rathus & Miller, 2014) and/or the DBT in Schools book (Mazza et al., 2016). It is our strong recommendation that thorough self-study and/or training in the DBT skills be conducted prior to implementing the interventions in this book in order to ensure a full understanding of the concepts being taught.

Unit One

PRINCIPLES OF DIALECTICS

Dialectical Behavioral Therapy grounds itself in the concept of dialectics, or thinking and acting in ways that are dialectical. So what the heck does being dialectical mean? Being dialectical is the practice of recognizing that there are no absolute truths; that there are multiple perspectives in any given moment or situation, sometimes polar opposite perspectives, and that any of these perspectives can be true at the same time. To be dialectical means having the ability to see different sides of a matter in search of a synthesis. A common example of practicing dialectics includes loving Winter while hating having to shovel snow, or being able to see the wisdom in a child's sadness that they failed a test even if you are feeling frustrated knowing that they didn't study.

Allowing themself to be dialectical helps a person stay away from extremes through searching for a middle ground that incorporates multiple perspectives. Adopting this way of thinking can make it easier to resolve disagreements, see other people's points of view, and search for a resolution. Four core concepts guide dialectics:

- opposites fill the universe
- connection surrounds all people, places, and things
- change happens and one can learn to embrace it
- the transactional nature of change.

The exercises and activities found in this unit explore the concept of dialectics, reminding us of our connection to one another, and allowing us to practice willingness to change.

17

✿ OPPOSITES!

Module: General Skills

Skill addressed
Dialectics

Summary
The main goal is to define the word "dialectics" and identify opposites in our world.

Materials needed

◆   Video or audio of the song "That's What Makes the World Go Round" from the Disney movie *The Sword in the Stone* (1963) and the means to play the video/audio

Lesson preparation

◆   Cue video/audio
◆   List several opposites on the board: Right—Left; Up—Down, etc.

Lesson overview

1.   Explain dialectics as "the world is made of opposites. These opposites help our world keep growing and changing."
2.   Ask students to listen to the song and pay attention to the opposites they hear.
3.   Play the song for the students and add opposites to the list on the board.
4.   Introduce movements (see the movements provided) of the song to the students.
5.   Play the song and model the movements along with the students.
6.   Discussion questions:
     ▪   Could you follow along with the opposites in the song?
     ▪   What is the opposite of up?
     ▪   What is the opposite of in?
     ▪   Can you think of any other opposites?
     ▪   Is it important that we have opposites like both "stop" and "go"?

Modifications for higher developmental level

1. Ask the students to create a list of opposites on the board.
2. Explain dialectics as "the world is made of opposites. These opposites help our world keep growing and changing."
3. Teach the movements of the song.
4. Play the song and ask the students to use the movements they have learned during the video.
5. Discussion questions:
   - The song says "opposites make the world go round"—what does that mean?
   - Are people always right or always wrong?
   - Is lemonade just sweet or just sour?
   - When you jump do you go up or down?
   - Why is it important to see opposite sides of a situation?
   - Can you think of a situation in which seeing the opposite helped you understand someone else better?
   - What would happen if everyone always had the same thoughts and opinions?
6. Last thoughts to share with students:
   - Opposites allow us to explore different points of view
   - Opposites allow us to solve problems in many ways
   - Opposites exist together to create wonderful results—great lemonade is sweet and sour

Use these movements as you listen to the chorus of the song

Left and right: Hold up left hand then right hand

Day and night: Circle hand over head then hands by face in a sleeping pose

In and out: Hands point toward self for "in" then open out for "out"

Thin and stout: Bring hands together then bring hands apart

Up and down: Point up then point down

Square and round: Draw a square then draw a circle

High and low: Point up then point down

To and fro: Rock side to side moving left then right

Stop and go: Hold up hand with palm facing forward to "stop" then point forward for "go"

MOVE MY STATUE

Module: General Skills

Skill addressed

Dialectics: Change

Summary

The main goal of this activity is to practice change.

Materials needed

- Song "Change the Way" by Ellie Lawson or another song about change and the means to play the song

Lesson preparation

- Cue audio
- Separate class into groups of three or four

Lesson overview

1. Have students stand in their groups.
2. All but one student are asked to pose like a statue.
3. Start the music. While the song plays, the non-statue goes through and tells the statues in their group how to change. For example: sit down, raise your left hand, turn around.
4. Repeat until all children get to be the "change director."
5. Discussion questions:
   - What was it like when you were asked to change?
   - What was it like for you to have to change others?
   - Is changing always easy?

Modifications for higher developmental level

LESSON PREPARATION

- Pair students

LESSON OVERVIEW

1. Have students face their partner.
2. One student is asked to pose like a statue.
3. Start the music. While the song plays, the other student poses differently and the first statue has to match them.
4. Repeat several rounds taking turns being the leader and the follower/ student that needs to change.
5. Discussion questions:
   - How did you feel when you needed to change?
   - Was it harder to be a changing statue or the student changing the statue?
   - Is change always easy?
   - Why is it important to practice change?

�֍ DRAW AND DESCRIBE

Module: General Skills

Skill addressed
Dialectics: Truth in different interpretations

Summary
The main goal of this activity is to allow students to experience music creatively and recognize similarity and differences in interpretations.

Materials needed

- Various recordings of instrumental music and means to play the recordings
- Paper, colored pencils, crayons

Lesson preparation

- Cue up audio
- Have paper, colored pencils, and crayons ready for use

Lesson overview

1. Instruct students to lay out several colored pencils or crayons in front of them and a piece of paper.
2. Ask the students to close their eyes and listen to the music while thinking about the music in color—"what colors can they imagine in this music?"
3. At the end of the song, instruct the students to open their eyes and gather the colors they imagined in the music.
4. Ask the students to draw whatever comes to mind—shapes, images, etc.—using the colors they pictured.
5. Compare and discuss similarities and differences in their pictures.
6. Reinforce the question "Who is right?" The answer, of course, being "everyone."

Modifications for higher developmental level

1. Instruct students to lay out several colored pencils or crayons in front of them and a piece of paper.
2. Ask the students to close their eyes and listen to the music while thinking about the music in color—"what colors can they imagine in this music?"
3. At the end of the song, instruct the students to open their eyes and gather the colors they imagined in the music.
4. Ask the students to draw whatever comes to mind—shapes, images, words, emotions—with those colors.
5. Repeat with two additional songs.
6. Gather students in groups of three or four.
7. Compare and discuss similarities and differences in their pictures.
8. Reinforce the question "Who is right?" The answer, of course, being "everyone."
9. Challenge students to "describe" another student's picture to the class.

MINDFULNESS

Mindfulness helps us learn how to pay attention in the moment with intention and purpose. Developmentally, the ability to stop and notice one's inner experiences and the world around us actively forms in early childhood. It is the set of skills upon which all of the other DBT skills rely; i.e., one must be able to observe their emotions and corresponding action urges before figuring out how to act differently, connect to others, and manage intense moments. Mindfulness skills therefore aim to build upon and enhance this growing ability in children.

This unit includes activities for the following DBT mindfulness skills: Wise Mind, the "What" Skills: Observe, Describe, and Participate, and the "How" Skills: Don't Judge, Stay Focused, Do What Works.

Mindfulness experiences are often incorporated at the beginning of every DBT lesson. As noted above, mindfulness abilities are just starting to develop at the elementary level so repetition is necessary and encouraged. Thus, we have included multiple interventions for the concepts in this unit so that there are many options to use for teaching, and reinforcing, mindfulness skills.

A FEW HELPFUL CLASSROOM MINDFULNESS TIPS

- Say "be mindful" instead of "pay attention" or "listen."
- Start and end the day and exercises with a simple breathing technique. For example:
  - Square breathing using the desk: Have the students use their pointer finger and start at the corner of their desk—breathe in as they trace the side, breathe out as they make the turn across the

back of the desk, breathe in as they trace the other side of the desk towards them, and breathe out as they go across the bottom.

- Draw an arch on the board—breathe in from one end of the arch to the other end "of the rainbow" and release.
- Play a bell, breathing in with sound and out as the sound fades away.
- Place your hands on the desk and feet on the floor—deep breathe in and out.
- 4-4-4. Breathe in for count of 4, hold for 4, out for 4.

❀ MINDFULNESS

Module: Mindfulness

Skill addressed
General mindfulness

Summary
The main goal of this activity is for children to focus their attention mindfully in the moment while breathing to the cues in the song.

Materials needed

◆ Lyrics and recorded song "Mindfully Here and Now" or some sort of soothing background music and the means to play the recording (recording available at https://www.youtube.com/playlist?list=PL0jguhoPs0m 6qrlhhTR7P4PPtz7wuicy1 or by scanning the QR code in the Appendix)

Lesson preparation

◆ Cue audio
◆ Write the lyrics on board

Lesson overview

1. Say, "Mindfulness is paying attention on purpose. We will listen to the instructions in this song and pay attention to what the instructions tell you to notice."
2. Ask students to sit with feet on the floor and eyes down.
3. Ask them to listen carefully to the song.
4. Play the recording of the following song, or, instead of singing or listening to the song, you can play quiet music and read the lyrics.
5. Discussion questions:
   ▪ What did you notice during the song?
   ▪ Could you take a slow, deep breath the next time you wanted to focus?

Verse 1:
Feeling your feet on the floor
Feel the air on your skin

Notice how your body feels
As you breathe out and breathe in

Chorus:
Breathe in, And out, Breathe in, And out, Breathe in, And out, Mindfully
here and now

Verse 2:
Now take a look all around.
What do you see?
Mindfully see what you see as you breathe out and breathe in.

Chorus:
Breathe in, And out, Breathe in, And out, Breathe in, And out, Mindfully
here and now

Verse 3:
Now in the quiet
Listen,
…What do you hear?
Mindfully listen as you breathe out and breathe in

Chorus:
Breathe in, And out, Breathe in, And out, Breathe in, And out, Mindfully
here and now

Verse 4:
What do you feel inside?
Observe and focus within.
Relax now, and just let it be
As you breathe out and breathe in

Chorus:
Breathe in, And out, Breathe in, And out, Breathe in, And out, Mindfully
here and now

❀ MUSICAL STATES OF MIND

Module: Mindfulness

Skill addressed
Wise Mind

Summary
The main goal of this exercise is to teach and identify the three states of mind: reasonable, emotional, and wise mind.

Materials needed

◆ A march, for example "The Washington Post" by J. Philip Sousa, and the means to play the audio
◆ Whiteboard or large piece of paper to write on
◆ Appropriate writing utensil

Lesson preparation

◆ Draw a Venn diagram on the board or large piece of paper
◆ Label the circles from left to right: reasonable mind, wise mind (in the overlap), emotion mind

Lesson overview

1. Have the students stand up.
2. Play the march and ask the students to march like robots.
3. Teach: There are three "states of mind."
   ▪ Reasonable mind is ruled by facts and logic. It is like a robot that feels no emotion.
4. Play the march again and allow the students to "jump up and down" without touching anyone or hurting themselves for one minute.
5. Teach: There are three "states of mind."
   ▪ Emotion mind is ruled by feelings and urges. It is like a tornado that doesn't care about rules.
6. Ask: "How can you bring them together?" Ask the students to stand and move to the music any way they wish but they must stay in a line.

- Wise mind allows us to play by the rules but also have some fun. When we are wise, we listen and try to make helpful choices.

Modifications for higher developmental level

1. Have the students stand up.
2. Play the march and ask the students to march like robots.
3. Teach: There are three "states of mind."
   - Reasonable mind is ruled by facts and logic. It is like a robot that feels no emotion. In reasonable mind you think about facts, research at the library or online for example, or a scientist. Let's say you were searching for a new item. You compare the various types of that item and cost. You analyse the various items and select the best one.
4. Play the march again and allow the students to "dance in place" without touching anyone or hurting themselves for one minute.
5. Teach: There are three "states of mind."
   - Emotion mind is ruled by feelings and urges. It is like a tornado that doesn't care about rules. When you're in this state of mind we tend to act without thinking first. For example if you are mad you might yell or throw something or do something that gets you in trouble.
6. Ask: "How can you bring them together?" Ask them to stand and move to the music any way they wish but stay in a line.
7. Teach: There are three "states of mind."
   - Wise mind allows us to play by the rules but have some fun too. When we are wise, we listen and try to make helpful choices. In wise mind, we are aware of both the facts and reason as well as our urges of emotion. This is where we do what we know and feel is right.
8. Discussion questions:
   - Can you name a time you had to investigate something like a scientist in reasonable mind?
   - Can you name a time you did something without thinking like in emotion mind?
   - Can you name a time that you know you did the helpful/"right" thing and acted in wise mind?

✿ NOTICE MY BREATH

Module: Mindfulness

Skill addressed
"What" Skill: Observe

Summary
The main goal of this activity is to practice awareness and take breaths guided by song.

Materials needed

◆ Video of the song "Notice My Breath" by Chelsea Steen and means to play the video (recording available at https://www.youtube.com/playlist?list =PL0jguhoPs0m6qrlhhTR7P4PPtz7wuicy1 or by scanning the QR code in the Appendix)

Lesson preparation

◆ Cue video

Lesson overview

1. Introduce the idea of observing your body by focusing on the breath.
2. Explain that thinking about each part of your body one at a time can be a way to observe how you feel.
3. Demonstrate and model breathing, then practice with the students.
4. Instruct the students to follow the directions for breathing in the song.
5. Play through the song one or two times for students to breathe along and notice body parts.
6. Discussion questions:
   - Did your mind get distracted while listening to the song?
   - Could you bring it back to take deep breaths?
   - What body part could you focus on the best?
   - What body part was hard to focus on?
   - What did you notice when you took a breath?

✿ CATCH THE BREATH

Module: Mindfulness

Skill addressed
"What" Skill: Observe

Summary
The main goal of this activity is to observe and practice our breath.

Materials needed

◆ Recording of a song such as "Breathin'" by Ariana Grande or "Breathe Again" by Toni Braxton that includes the word breath and means to play the song (**Note:** make sure you use the radio edit version, so the lyrics are school appropriate)

Lesson preparation

◆ Have the song cued and ready to play

Lesson overview

1. Instruct the students to raise their hands each time the singer says any form of "breathe" or "breath." The teacher keeps a tally on the board.
2. At the end of the song, say "we were being mindful and observing the words 'breath' and 'breathe.'"
3. Ask the class to practice breathing slowly eight times. They could utilize their hands going out and in to help direct the breath. For example, hold arms bent toward chest—as breathing in extend arms open, and as breathing out curl arms closed toward body.

Modifications for higher developmental levels

1. Instruct the students to raise their hands each time the singer says any form of "breathe" or "breath." The teacher (or choose a student) keeps a tally on their paper.
2. At the end of the song, say "we were being mindful and observing the words 'breath' and 'breathe.'"

3. Ask: "How many students counted the correct number of times?"
4. Teach various breathing strategies that can be practiced throughout the week:
    - Square breathing—breathe in as you trace up the side of a rectangle shape (box); breathe out as you trace across the top; breathe in as you trace down the other side; breathe out across the bottom
    - Breath counting—breathe in to count of 4 and out to count of 8
    - "Trace the Hand"—take pointer finger and trace up the other hand, breathe in as you trace up the thumb; breathe out from tip to crease with pointer finger; breathe in as you trace up the pointer; breathe out as you move to the crease with the middle finger; etc.

❀ RAINBOW

Module: Mindfulness

Skill addressed
"What" Skill: Observe

Summary
The main goal of this activity is to practice observing through finding each of the colors of the rainbow.

Materials needed

- Video of the song "Rainbow" by Chelsea Steen and means to play the video (recording available at https://www.youtube.com/playlist?list=PL0 jguhoPs0m6qrlhhTR7P4PPtz7wuicy1 or by scanning the QR code in the Appendix)

Lesson preparation

- Cue video

Lesson overview

1. Introduce the idea of observing the room you are in and looking for different colors.
2. Explain that in the song, each of the colors of the rainbow will be sung and the color shown on the video. One for red, orange, yellow, green, blue, and purple.
3. Play the video showing the picture of the color paired with each verse of the song.
4. Depending on the size of the group, children can point to or name out loud the object of each color.
5. Play the video and pause between colors if needed.
6. Discussion questions:
   - Could you find something of every color?
   - Do you notice the colors around you at school? At home?
   - Can you remember the song to name the colors of the rainbow?
   - Do you have a favorite color that you notice in every room you go?

Modifications for higher developmental level

1. Introduce the idea of observing the room you are in and looking for different colors.

2. Explain that in the song each of the colors of the rainbow will be sung and the color shown on the video. One for red, orange, yellow, green, blue, and purple.

3. Play the video showing the picture of the color paired with each verse of the song.

4. Play the video and ask the students to choose one color and find at least three items in the room that match that color.

5. Ask the students to observe and share the items and one additional aspect of the object they observe, for example "the ball is red and it is round."

6. Discussion questions:
   - Could you find something of every color?
   - Do you notice the colors around you at school? At home?
   - When you notice the colors and features of an item, what does that help you do?

❀ USE MY SENSES

Module: Mindfulness

Skill addressed
"What" Skill: Observe

Summary
The main goal of this activity is to practice observing the world through the five senses.

Materials needed

- Lyrics for "Use My Senses" by Chelsea Steen (included in lesson overview)
- Video for "Use My Senses" by Chelsea Steen (recording available at https://www.youtube.com/playlist?list=PL0jguhoPs0m6qrlhhTR7P4P Ptz7wuicy1 or by scanning the QR code in the Appendix)
- Optional: instrumental of "Twinkle, Twinkle, Little Star" and means to play the audio
- Items in the room to see, touch, hear, smell, taste

Lesson preparation

- Cue audio if using
- Write the lyrics on the board
- Ensure items available in the room for each sense

Lesson overview

1. Explain that we can notice the world around us through five senses. When noticing, it is called "observing." Have children name the five senses.
2. Sing the following adapted lyrics to the tune of "Twinkle, Twinkle, Little Star."

   When I feel out of control,
   I know just where to go.
   I think about my five senses,
   Brings me back to feeling calm.
   My eyes see, my ears hear,

my nose can smell.
My mouth tastes,
and my hands can touch.

Notice one thing that I see: .... *(pause)*
Notice one thing that I hear: .... *(pause)*
Notice one thing that I smell:............. *(pause)*
Notice one thing that I taste: .... *(pause)*
Notice one thing that I touch:............. *(pause)*
Brings me back to feeling calm.

3. Pause after each of the five senses and ask children to name an item for each category.
4. Discussion questions:
   - What was the easiest item to find?
   - What was the hardest item to find?
   - Was there one you liked best?
   - Was there any you did not like?

Modifications for higher developmental level
LESSON PREPARATION

- Write the lyrics on the board
- Ensure items available in the room for each sense
- Find a rap background beat using a keyboard with a rhythm function, garage band, or a background beat from the internet

LESSON OVERVIEW

1. Explain that we can notice the world around us through five senses. When noticing, it is called "observing." Have children name the five senses.
2. Rap the following adapted lyrics along with the background beat. A framework tune is "Twinkle, Twinkle, Little Star"

When I feel out of control,
I know just where to go.
I think about my five senses,
Brings me back to feeling calm.
My eyes see, my ears hear,

my nose can smell.
My mouth tastes,
and my hands can touch.

Notice one thing that I see:. . . . . (pause)
Notice one thing that I hear: . . . . (pause)
Notice one thing that I smell:. . . . . (pause)
Notice one thing that I taste: . . . . (pause)
Notice one thing that I touch:. . . . . (pause)
Brings me back to feeling calm.

3. Repeat additional times for children to find up to three items for each of the senses.

THE TRAIN

Module: Mindfulness

Skill addressed

"What" Skill: Describe

Summary

The main goal of this activity is to describe five facts about their own drawing of a train.

Materials needed

- Recording of "Train is a-coming" by Pete Seeger and means to play the audio
- Paper, colored pencils, crayons
- Various pictures of trains

Lesson preparation

- Cue audio
- Pass out blank pieces of paper and your choice of markers, crayons, colored pencils

Lesson overview

1. Explain that when we observe something and then use words to talk about it, we are using the skill: "describe."
2. Invite children to listen to the song about a train. Explain: "As you listen, you will draw a picture of a train. You can draw the train in any way that you want."
3. If needed, offer a few pictures of different kinds of trains so children have an idea of what they look like.
4. Play the recorded song "Train is a-coming." Offer more time for children to finish their picture by playing the song two or three times.
5. After the pictures are drawn, ask children to think of five words to describe their picture. This can be done in small groups of students or with the entire group. If needed, prompt with options such as the following:
   - How many cars did you draw?

- What color did you use?
- How many wheels does it have?
- Are there people on your train?
- Is there decoration on the train?
- Does it have windows?
- Is it carrying anything?

6. Discussion questions:
   - Have you ever seen a train before?
   - Could you think of five facts about your picture?
   - Could your friend see everything you described in your picture?
   - Did you have enough time to add everything you wanted on your train?

Modifications for higher developmental level

1. Explain that when we observe something and then use words to talk about it, we are using the skill "describe."
2. Invite children to listen to the song about a train. Explain: "As you listen, you will draw a picture of a train. You can draw the train in any way that you want."
3. Play the recorded song "Train is a-coming." Offer more time for children to finish their picture by playing the song two or three times.
4. After the pictures are drawn, pair children and have them write down five facts about their partner's train.
5. Have each child present their partner's drawing and describe the facts to the group.

❀ I LIKE THE FLOWERS

Module: Mindfulness

Skill addressed
"What" Skill: Participate

Summary
The main goal of this activity is to participate fully through singing and following the lap-clap pattern.

Materials needed

♦ Audio of the traditional folk song "I Like the Flowers" and the means to play it or option to sing a cappella

Lesson preparation

♦ Cue audio
♦ Write lyrics on board

Lesson overview

1. Ask what it means to "participate"—to do an activity fully.
2. Show the body percussion pattern of tapping knees with hands and then clapping.
3. Class practices without music.
4. Start the song or begin singing the lyrics of the song, modeling the pattern of tapping knees with hands and then clapping.

The following is the traditional folk song "I Like the Flowers"

(Lap)   (Clap)
I like flowers

(Lap)   (Clap)
I like the daffodils

(Lap)   (Clap)
I like the mountains

(Lap)   (Clap)
I like the rolling hills

(Lap)   (Clap)
I like the fireside

(Lap)   (Clap)
When all the lights are low

(Lap)   (Clap)
Boom de-ahh-da Boom de-ahh-da

(Lap)   (Clap)
Boom de-ahh-da Boom de- ay

(Lap)   (Clap)
Boom de-ahh-da Boom de-ahh-da

(Lap)   (Clap)
Boom de-ahh-da Boom de-ay

5. Discussion questions:
   - Did you participate throughout the song?
   - Did you have to remind yourself to keep tapping and clapping?
   - Could you sing and clap at the same time?
   - What else did you notice?
   - What was hard about it? What was easy about it?

Modifications for higher developmental level
MATERIALS NEEDED

- Audio of "We Will Rock You" by Queen and means to play it or option to sing a cappella
- Lyrics to the song on the whiteboard

LESSON OVERVIEW

1. Ask what it means to "participate"—to do an activity fully.
2. Show the body percussion pattern of tapping knees with hands and then clapping: TAP—TAP—CLAP.
3. The class should practice without music.
4. Start the song or begin singing the lyrics of the song, modeling the pattern of tapping knees with hands and then clapping.
5. Choose from the discussion questions:
   - Did you participate throughout the song?
   - Did you have to remind yourself to keep tapping and clapping?
   - Could you sing and clap at the same time?
   - What else did you notice? Did you notice any emotions come up in you? Any thoughts running through your mind?
   - What was hard about it? What was easy about it?

✿ LISTEN FOR THE WORD

Module: Mindfulness

Skill addressed
"What" Skill: Participate

Summary
The main goal of this activity is to fully participate in the activity while letting go of distractions.

Materials needed

◆ Recording of a song with a frequently repeated word (e.g. "My Bonnie Lies Over the Ocean" or "Row Row Row Your Boat") and means to play the audio

Lesson preparation

◆ Cue audio

Lesson overview

1. Play music and instruct students to follow a directive when they hear the repeated word. For example:
   - Put your hand on your head
   - Touch your nose
   - Stand up/sit down.
2. Play music multiple times, changing the directive as time permits.
3. Discussion questions:
   - Was it easy to participate?
   - Was there a time where your mind wandered?
   - What did you do to pay attention?

Modifications for higher developmental level
MATERIALS NEEDED

◆ Recording of a song with a frequently repeated word (e.g. "Thunderstruck"

by AC/DC or "Thunder" by Imagine Dragons) and means to play the audio
- One object for each student to pass (e.g. balls, bean bags, cups, etc.)

LESSON PREPARATION

- Cue audio
- Set up room for students to sit in a circle

LESSON OVERVIEW

1. Have students sit in a circle. Give each student an object to pass.
2. Have students practice passing their object to the right.
3. Prompt students to pass only when they hear the specific repeated word in the song.
4. Repeat the exercise, however this time passing to the left.
5. Discussion questions:
   - What was difficult about this activity?
   - Was it easy to participate?
   - Was there a time where your mind wandered? If it did, what did it wander to?
   - What did you do to pay attention?

✿ NAME THAT INSTRUMENT

Module: Mindfulness

Skill addressed

"What" Skills: Observe, Describe, Participate

Summary

The main goal of this exercise is to observe, describe, and participate through exploring and/or creating various instruments. Each aspect of the "what" skills is done one at a time emphasizing observe, then describe, followed by participate.

Materials needed

- Tambourine
- Hand drum
- Shakers
- Craft materials to create "student made" instruments (e.g. paper plates, string, jingle bells (for tambourines), bucket lids (for drums), beans and water bottles (for shakers), keys)

Lesson overview

1. Play three instruments, asking the students to just listen and "observe." Explain: "We observe with our senses—our eyes, ears, nose, taste, and touch." Ask: "How did you observe the instruments?"
2. Play three instruments a second time and ask the students to "describe" the sound that each instrument made. Explain: "Describe is using words to share what you observed." Ask: "What made that sound different than the last? Use your ears and eyes to notice the similarities and differences."
3. Ask the students to pick an instrument to play. Allow them to play and explore the instrument: "Participate."
4. If time allows, practice paying attention on purpose through a game. Have the students hide their eyes or hide the instrument from their view and play. What was the sound? How did you know?
5. If time allows, ask the students to create their own instrument and repeat the first three steps with their own instrument.

Modifications for higher developmental level
LESSON PREPARATION

- Expand number and types of instruments utilized
- Ask students to bring in materials from home that they can use to create their own instruments

LESSON OVERVIEW

1. Play three instruments asking the students to just listen and "observe." Explain: "We observe with our senses—our eyes, ears, nose, taste, and touch." Ask: "How did you observe the instruments?"
2. Play three instruments a second time and ask the students to "describe" the sound that each instrument made. Explain: "Describe is using words to share what you observed." Ask: "What made that sound different than the last? Use your ears and eyes to notice the similarities and differences."
3. Ask the students to pick an instrument to play. Allow them to play and explore the instrument. "Participate."
4. If time allows, practice paying attention on purpose through a game. Have the students hide their eyes or hide the instrument from their view and play. What was the sound? How did you know?
5. If time allows, ask the students to create their own instrument and repeat the first three steps with their own instrument.

❀ SONG LISTENING

Module: Mindfulness

Skill addressed
"What" Skills: Observe, Describe, Participate

Summary
The main goal of this exercise is to observe, describe, and participate while listening to a piece of music. Each aspect of the "what" skills is done one at a time emphasizing observe, then describe, followed by participate.

Materials needed

- Recording of a song with a positive message that your students enjoy and means to play the audio

Lesson preparation

- Cue audio
- Write "Observe, Describe, Participate" on the board

Lesson overview

1. Share with students: "Today we are going to practice mindfulness through listening to a song three times. Each time we will practice one step. The steps are:
   - Observe
   - Describe
   - Participate."
2. "First, we are just going to listen, notice, and **observe** the song." Play the song.
3. "Now, we are going to listen and then **describe** one thing you noticed about the song." Play the song the second time and ask the students to describe one thing they noticed after listening.
4. "Lastly, we are going to **participate**." Prompt the students to clap along, tap their toes, and sway in their seats. Play the song for the third time, encouraging them to participate in some way (sing, clap, snap, tap toes).

Modifications for higher developmental level

MATERIALS NEEDED

- Recording of a song with a positive message that your students enjoy and means to play the audio
- Speaker
- Typed out lyric sheets
- Appropriate writing utensil

LESSON PREPARATION

- Have song cued
- Write "Observe, Describe, Participate" on the board
- Print off a lyric sheet for each student

LESSON OVERVIEW

1. Explain: "Today we are going to practice the three steps of the mindfulness 'what' skills." Share:
   - Observe means noticing
   - Describe is using words to share facts about what we observed
   - Participate is when we engage in an experience.
2. Explain: "We are going to listen to this song three times. First we're going to just listen." Play your selected song for the students and ask students to just listen and **observe.**
3. "Now we will listen again and **describe** what you observe by writing it down. Remember descriptions are facts; for example: the music was fast, I heard a guitar. Consider lyrics, the speed, instruments, and anything else that you notice."
   - Invite a short discussion on what the students described on their paper.
4. Next, distribute the lyrics: "This time, you will practice **participating.** As you listen and follow the lyrics, underline your favorite line in the song."
5. Invite students to share their favorite line.
6. Discussion questions:
   - What was easy or hard about just observing?
   - Were you able to describe using just facts?
   - Did you do the activity? If so, you participated! What did you notice when you were participating?

❀ DANCE IT OUT

Module: Mindfulness

Skill addressed
"How" Skill: Stay Focused

Summary
The main goal of this exercise is to follow directions by paying attention and doing just one thing at a time.

Materials needed

- Recorded music that has dance directives in the song (e.g. "Head, Shoulders, Knees and Toes" or "The Hokey Pokey") and means to play the audio

Lesson preparation

- Cue audio
- Have the words "Stay Focused" written on the board

Lesson overview

1. Explain: "We are going to listen to a song. Your job is to listen and follow each direction exactly as you hear it."
2. Invite the students to get ready to dance.
3. Play the song and follow the directions in the song.
4. Discussion questions:
   - Is it challenging to do one thing at a time?
   - What if I asked you to jump up and down, turn around, touch your toes, and wiggle your fingers all at the same time? Would it be very hard?
   - Reinforce that when we do one thing at a time it is easier and important to practice.
5. Repeat to practice "staying focused."

Modifications for higher developmental level
MATERIALS NEEDED

- Recorded music that has dance directives in the song like "Cha Cha Slide" by DJ Casper or "Cupid Shuffle" by Cupid and means to play the audio
- A bell or way to create a sound to add distraction

LESSON PREPARATION

- Cue audio
- Have the words "Stay focused" written on the board

LESSON OVERVIEW

1. Explain: "We are going to listen to a song. Your job is to listen and follow each direction exactly as you hear it."
2. Invite the students to get ready to dance.
3. After the song ends, ask the students to repeat the dance. This time add in a distraction sound, for example loud talking over the song, clapping, singing, ringing a bell.
4. Discussion questions:
   - Was it challenging to follow the steps?
   - Could you follow the directions when I was making all the extra sounds?

❀ MUSICAL WORKOUT

Module: Mindfulness

Skill addressed
"How" Skill: Stay Focused

Summary
The main goal of this activity is to practice doing one thing at a time.

Materials needed

+ A selected favorite classroom-friendly song and the means to play it
+ Timer
+ A six-sided die

Lesson preparation

+ Cue audio
+ Assign an exercise to each number of the die and write on the board. For example:
  1. Stretch tall
  2. Shrug shoulders
  3. Arm circles
  4. Jumping jacks
  5. Bend forward
  6. Stand on tippy toes
+ Know how to properly and safely execute each physical exercise

Lesson overview

1. Explain: "We will roll the die and see what exercise we will do. Each exercise will be done for the selected amount of time (e.g. 30 seconds)."
2. Ask a student to roll the die and follow the selected exercise.
3. Demonstrate exercise as needed.
4. Prompt the students to continue exercise/movement until the timer stops.
5. Discussion questions:
   - What was easy about this activity?
   - What was hard about this activity?

- Were you able to just do one exercise at a time?
- Was it easy to focus on just yourself? Did you have to pay attention to others?

Modifications for higher developmental level
LESSON PREPARATION

- Have the students assign an exercise or favorite dance move to each number of the dice. For example:
  1. Stretching tall
  2. Shrug shoulder
  3. Arm circles
  4. Jumping jacks
  5. Bend forward
  6. Running in place
- Cue up a favorite classroom song
- Know how to properly and safely execute each physical exercise

LESSON OVERVIEW

1. Explain: "We will roll the dice and see what exercise we will do. Do as many reps of the exercise as you can in one minute (or whatever amount of time you select)."
2. Ask students to take turns selecting an exercise by rolling the dice and following the key created on the board.
3. Demonstrate the exercise if needed.
4. Reinforce staying on that one exercise until the timer stops: if you feel like stopping, try not to; if you absolutely must, take a break.
5. Next, have the students roll multiple dice and do the exercises in that order.
6. Discussion questions:
   - How did you follow along and know what to do?
   - Was it easy to stay focused on one exercise?
   - When would it be helpful to only focus on one thing?
   - When you started to get tired did you stop or did you keep going and cheer yourself on?
   - Was it harder to keep track of the exercises as we added more exercises to the routine?

❀ ROW, ROW, FACT OR FOE

Module: Mindfulness

Skill addressed
"How" Skill: Don't Judge

Summary
The main goal of this activity is to identify the difference between fact and opinion.

Materials needed

◆ Print out the new lyrics to be sung to the tune "Row Row Row Your Boat" or write on board

◆ Pictures of items or actual objects, approximately ten items (include a variety of things—paper clip, red pen, box of crayons, maraca, chair, an apple, a lamp, a pillow, table, a book, etc.)

Lesson preparation

◆ Write new lyrics to "Row Row Row Your Boat" on the whiteboard

Lesson overview

1. Explain to students there is a difference between a statement that is a fact and one that is an opinion.
2. A fact is something that is true and doesn't change, and an opinion is a belief that may be different from someone else's.
3. Sing the following lyrics to the tune of "Row Row Row Your Boat":

> *A fact is something that is true*
> *I cannot change it.*
> *Opinion is what I think,*
> *My friend might think differently.*

4. Explain: "We will look at different pictures (or objects) and I will say a statement that is either a fact or an opinion. You will then tell me if what I said is a fact or opinion."

5. Sing the following lyrics to the tune "Row Row Row Your Boat":

Fact or opinion
Which one will it be?
Look at the picture
What do you see?
Tell your teacher please...

6. Present an object or picture and make a statement about it. Between each example sing both sections of the song to practice the definition of fact and opinion. Invite students to join in singing. Examples:
    - Show a paperclip: "This paperclip is silver" (fact)
    - Show a red pen: "This pen is red" (fact)
    - Show an apple: "Apples are the best" (opinion) "This apple is red" (fact)
    - Show a picture of a cat: "This cat is cute" (opinion)
    - Show a picture of a snake: "Snakes are scary" (opinion)
    - Show a picture of a green snake: "This snake is green" (fact)
    - Show a picture of grapes: "Grapes are gross" (opinion)
    - Show a blue pillow: "This pillow is soft" (fact)
    - Show a wooden chair: "This chair is made of wood" (fact)
    - Show a picture of a puppy: "Puppies are my favorite" (opinion).
7. Discussion questions:
    - What is a fact?
    - What is an opinion?
    - Do you ever have opinions that are different from your friends?

Modifications for higher developmental level

1. Explain to students there is a difference between a statement that is a fact and one that is an opinion.
2. A fact is something that is true and doesn't change, and an opinion is a belief that may be different from someone else's.
3. Sing the following lyrics to the tune of "Row Row Row Your Boat":

A fact is something that is true
I cannot change it.
Opinion is what I think,
My friend might think differently.

4. The teacher picks up an object and states one fact about it and one opinion. Sing the tune again reinforcing the definitions.
5. Ask each student to pick an object from the room and write down one fact and one opinion.
6. Ask students to share and, depending on the size of your class, sing the tune after every student or every three to five students have shared. Invite the students to join in singing—challenge the class to sing it in a round.

Fact or opinion
Which one will it be?
Look at the picture
What do you see?
Tell your teacher please…

7. Discussion questions:
   - What is a fact?
   - What is an opinion?
   - Do you ever have opinions that are different from your friends?
   - Can you think of a time when you thought something was a fact but it was actually an opinion?
   - Could you easily tell if it was fact or opinion?

⚘ NEW MOVES

Module: Mindfulness

Skill addressed
"How" Skill: Do What Works

Summary
The main goal of this activity is to focus on what works versus what is exactly right when learning something new through body movement.

Materials needed

♦ Recorded music with a strong beat (can be of student choice as appropriate) (e.g. "Happy" by Pharrell Williams; "In the Hall of the Mountain King" by Edvard Grieg) and means to play the audio

Lesson preparation

♦ Cue audio
♦ Have the word "Mindfulness" and and the phrase "Do What Works: Reach Your Goal" written on the board

Lesson overview

1. Explain: "We are going to work on learning how to snap our fingers. Take your 'Tall Finger' and your thumb and rub them together and soon they make a sound!"
2. Get ready to snap to a chosen song—try slow at first, then medium speed, then faster.
3. Discussion questions:
   - Were you able to get it right away?
   - Did anyone get frustrated trying to snap?
   - If you couldn't get the snap, what are some ways we could change it so that we are still able to make a sound with our fingers? (i.e. use flicking fingers, or just tap fingers together.)
4. Next, invite the students to try the song again, choosing to snap or make another sound with their fingers.

5. Discussion questions:
    ▪ Even if you couldn't snap, could you still make a sound?
    ▪ Sometimes even if we can't do something perfectly, it doesn't mean we can't do it. Can you think of a time you had to change the way you did something but you still accomplished your goal?

Modifications for higher developmental level
MATERIALS NEEDED

◆ Recorded music with a strong beat (can be of student choice as appropriate) (e.g. "Happy" by Pharrell Williams, "In the Hall of the Mountain King" by Edvard Grieg) and means to play the audio

LESSON PREPARATION

◆ Cue audio
◆ Have the word "Mindfulness" and the phrase "Do What Works: Successful in producing a desired or intended result" written on the board.

LESSON OVERVIEW

1. Have the students create five dance steps.
2. Put the students in groups of four and use the dance steps to create a routine they can do for the class.
3. Try learning the whole thing all at once, then break it down and try to learn just a part of the song.
4. Discussion questions:
    ▪ Was it easier to learn the whole dance routine in steps or all at once?
    ▪ Did you have to change during the song—especially as the music got faster?
    ▪ When you are working towards a goal—is it okay to change how you get there as long as you are successful?

ROLLER COASTER RIDE

Module: Mindfulness

Skill addressed

Skill review: Wise Mind; "What" Skills—Observe, Describe, Participate

Summary

The main goal of the lyrics of this song is to teach how to return to wise mind when on the road to impulsivity through practicing the "What" skills.

Materials needed

- Lyrics to the song "The Roller Coaster Ride" (included in the lesson overview)
- Recording of the song and means to play it (available at https://www.youtube.com/playlist?list=PL0jguhoPs0m6qrlhhTR7P4PPtz7wuicy1 or by scanning the QR code in the Appendix)

Lesson preparation

- Cue the song

Lesson overview

1. Explain: "When we get overwhelmed by our emotions, there is a point of no return (like a roller coaster) where we act impulsively, without any thought of consequences, and we don't even care. How can we get out of the grip of our emotions and make a wise choice about our behavior that won't leave us regretting something we did?"
2. Play the song for the class.
3. Discussion questions:
   - What emotions make you feel like you are on a roller coaster?
   - What are wise things you can do when you feel that way?

Modifications for higher developmental level

LESSON OVERVIEW

1. Explain: "When we get overwhelmed by our emotions, there is a point of

no return (a roller coaster) where we act impulsively, without any thought of consequences, and we don't even care. How can we get out of the grip of our emotions and make a wise choice about our behavior that won't leave us regretting something we did?"

2. Play the song all the way through.
3. Listen to the song again and stop the music in the places noted.

The Roller Coaster Ride
Somebody treated me unfair
I know I really shouldn't care
But I feel like doing something mean
I don't care if it's right or wrong

◆   Stop the music here and ask: "What mind am I in?" (emotion mind).

Oh, here comes the roller coaster ride
I feel the anger swell inside
It's not too late
To be wise

So emotions don't control me
I notice what's happening with me
Hot tears rolling down my face
My heart's beginning to race
My thoughts are those of revenge
Maybe I should relax with my friends instead

Oh, here comes the roller coaster ride
I feel the anger swell inside
It's not too late
To be wise

◆   Stop the music here and ask "What skill am I using?"
    ■   "Hot tears rolling down my face. My heart's beginning to race. My thoughts are those of revenge." (observe, describe)
◆   "How does it help to observe that I'm having the desire to get revenge before I act on that thought?"

Maybe I should go ride my bike

Or I could go for a hike
Walk outside and listen to the brook
Or maybe I could read a good book...
I could run real fast until the anger's gone
Or play guitar and sing you a song
Oh, here comes the roller coaster ride
I feel the anger swell inside
It's not too late
To be wise
It's not too late
To be wise

- "What does the singer do instead of getting revenge?"
- Make a list of ideas the students give you that would be good alternatives.

✿ LOVING KINDNESS

Module: Mindfulness

Skill addressed
Mindfulness review: "What" Skill: Participate; "How" Skills: Don't Judge and Do What Works

Summary
The main goal of this activity is to practice sharing without judging and doing what works with others through loving kindness.

Materials needed

◆ Recording of "I Wish You Peace" by The Eagles or a song that emphasizes kindness and means of playing the audio
◆ A copy of the lyrics so you can go through them with the students

Lesson overview

1. Explain: "Loving kindness is caring about others, ourselves, and even people we may not like. It helps us see the good in ourselves, others, and the world. We are going to listen to a song that can help us express this to ourselves and others."
2. Ask: "What are kind things you can say to others?" Make a list on the board.
3. Ask the students to pair up.
4. As the song plays, ask them to turn to a partner and wish them kind wishes.
5. Switch partners.
6. Listen to the song again and this time turn it into kind wishes for themselves.
7. Discussion questions:
   ▪ How did it feel to receive wishes of loving kindness?
   ▪ How do you think others feel when you give them wishes of loving kindness?

Modifications for higher developmental level

1. Explain: "Loving kindness is caring about others, ourselves, and even people we may not like. It helps us see the good in ourselves, others, and the world. We are going to listen to a song that can help us express this to ourselves and others."
2. Ask: "What are kind things you can say to others?" Make a list on the board.
3. Listen to the song.
4. Read through the lyrics of the first verses and discuss the lyrics.
5. During the guitar interlude, ask them to turn to a partner and wish them kind wishes.
6. Switch partners.
7. Listen to the song again and this time turn it into kind wishes for themselves.
8. Discussion questions:
   - How did it feel to receive wishes of loving kindness?
   - How do you think it helps others when you send them wishes of loving kindness?

✄ MINDFULNESS MONSTERS

Module: Mindfulness

Skill addressed
All mindfulness skills

Summary
The main goal of this activity is to review mindfulness skills creatively through developing a bulletin board of the students' work.

Materials needed

◆ Background music—challenge yourself to use spooky but fun songs, like "Monster Mash" by Bobby "Boris" Pickett & The Crypt Kickers—and means to play the music
◆ Construction paper, googly eyes, craft materials
◆ Paper, coloured pencils, crayons, etc.

Lesson preparation

◆ Cue audio
◆ Cut out shapes of friendly monsters
◆ Have mindfulness skills listed on the board or on small sheets of paper:
Wise Mind
Observe
Describe
Participate
Don't Judge
Stay Focused
Do What Works

Lesson overview

1. Ask the students to collect various supplies to create their own "Mindfulness Monster."
2. Play background music and as they are working pause every few minutes to review one of the mindfulness skills on the board.
3. Have each student select their favorite skill and add the label to their monster.
4. Have the students display their monster and skill on a bulletin board.

DISTRESS TOLERANCE

Distress tolerance skills give us the ability to get through situations where our emotions are very intense without making our situation worse by acting impulsively. Distressing situations happen to us all, and with distress tolerance skills we can learn how to get through those hard moments skillfully. Distress tolerance skills do not aim to change our emotions; they instead aim to give us options of other things we can do to buy ourselves time to bring down the intensity of our emotions and get our thinking brains back on track. Distress tolerance skills often need to happen before we can learn to regulate our emotions. If you can't think clearly because you're overwhelmed by emotion, it's going to be hard to try and change your emotions! STOP explores ways to slow our impulses. TIP addresses our body responses. Wise mind ACCEPTS offers productive distractions from our impulsive urges. PROS and CONS offers us a tool to explore outcomes and consequences. SELF SOOTHE uses our senses to comfort. Lastly, IMPROVE the moment challenges one to reframe thinking and behavior in the here and now to get through a moment with increased ease.

In addition to managing crisis moments, distress tolerance addresses reality when it isn't exactly the way we want it to be, and it may not be able to be changed. Radical acceptance, willingness versus wilfulness, and turning the mind skills help shape one's ability to get through these situations without making it worse.

A brief review of the acronyms utilized in the DBT Distress Tolerance module follows:

STOP:

Stop

Take a step back

Observe

Proceed mindfully

(Distracting with)

Wise mind ACCEPTS:

Activities

Contribution

Comparison

(with other) Emotions

Pushing away

(with other) Thoughts

Senses

TIP:

Temperature

Intense exercise

Paced breathing

Paired relaxation

IMPROVE the moment:

Imagery

Meaning

Prayer

Relaxing actions

One thing at a time

(a brief) Vacation

(self) Encouragement

✿ HEALTHY CHOICES FREEZE DANCE

Module: Distress Tolerance

Skill addressed
STOP

Summary
The main goal of this activity is to teach STOP while releasing energy, decreasing urges, encouraging self-control, and making healthier decisions.

Materials needed

- Recorded music with a good dance beat and means to play the audio
- Visual reminder—STOP sign on board
- Small stop signs with situations which require a healthy choice—situations can be adjusted for age group

Lesson preparation

- Cue audio
- Create five STOP Situations Cards on Index Cards with STOP Signs. Examples:

  Situation—You go to ride your bike and your friend is waiting, but you can't find your helmet.
  Choices—Do you go without it OR look for your helmet?
  Situation—You are hungry.
  Choices—Do you eat five cookies OR an apple and one cookie?
  Situation—You have homework to complete.
  Choices—Do you complete the five math problems you have to do or do you watch YouTube videos?
  Situation—It is five minutes until bedtime.
  Choices—Do you start a movie or brush your teeth?
  Situation—Your friend calls you a mean name.
  Choices—Do you punch your friend or walk away?

- Place five STOP sign cards on your desk

- On the board write:

Stop
Take a step back
Observe
Pick a healthy choice*

*Please note—This is a concrete adaptation from the typical *Proceed Mindfully*, which can be an abstract and more difficult concept for younger children.

Lesson overview

1. Introduce the concept of STOP to students by having them practice the STOP chant and movements.

   "Stop" (freeze your body)
   "Take a step back" (step backwards with feet)
   "Observe" (look both ways)
   "Pick a healthy choice" (hands open or a superhero stance such as hands on hips).

2. Invite the students to engage in a Freeze Dance game. When the music is playing, students can dance, move, and get some energy out. When the music stops, students will also stop and practice the STOP skill as shown in step 1.
3. Add the five STOP Situations you wrote on the index cards. Say: "When the music starts, listen closely as I am going to read you a situation."
4. Invite students to think about the situation and their choice in their head as you read a situation and the corresponding choices to the students.
5. Start music and dance.
6. Stop music and practice the STOP chant.
7. Invite students to raise their hand and tell you the "healthy choice" (OR have two lines on the floor—one specified for one choice, and one specified for the other. Have students move to the line that shows their choice).
8. Repeat multiple times with different situations and choices.

Modifications for higher developmental level

1. Invite students to identify a challenging situation they have had—use examples from the lesson preparation.
2. Have the students write a situation on an index card.
3. Introduce the concept of STOP to students by having them practice the STOP chant and movements.

   "Stop" (freeze your body)
   "Take a step back" (step backwards with feet)
   "Observe" (look both ways)
   "Pick a healthy choice" (hands open or a superhero stance such as hands on hips).

4. Invite the students to engage in a Freeze Dance game. When the music is playing, students can dance, move, and get some energy out. When the music stops, students will also stop and practice the STOP skill as shown in step 3.
5. Add the situations from the cards. Say: "When the music starts, listen close as I am going to read you a situation from our cards."
6. Invite students to think about the situation and their choice in their head as you read a situation and the corresponding choices to the students.
7. Start music and dance.
8. Stop music and practice the STOP chant.
9. Invite students to raise their hand and tell you "healthy choices" a person may have when facing the challenge that is read.
10. Repeat multiple times with different situations and choices.
11. Discussion questions:
    - How does STOP help us to make healthier choices?
    - Was it easy or hard to identify the healthy choice?
    - Was it easy or hard to make the healthy choice in the moment?
    - Has there been a time that you have made a choice that was not the "healthy" choice? What did you learn from that experience?

❀ STOP AND SING

Module: Distress Tolerance

Skill addressed
STOP

Summary
The main goal of this activity is to teach STOP while releasing energy, decreasing urges, encouraging self-control, and making healthier decisions.

Materials needed

* Visual of a STOP sign
* STOP written out with each step of the STOP skill after the corresponding letter:

Stop
Take a step back
Observe
Pick a healthy choice*
Lyrics of the STOP skill song (included in the lesson overview)

*Please note—This is a concrete adaptation from the typical *Proceed Mindfully*, which can be an abstract and more difficult concept for younger children.

Lesson overview

1. Show a stop sign and ask children if they know what it is.
2. State: "The STOP skill can help us to pause before acting so we can make a healthy choice."
3. Name the four steps of the STOP skill (pair with the letters of the word if appropriate for the children):
   * Stop
   * Take a step back
   * Observe
   * Pick a healthy choice.
4. State: "Today we will learn a song so we can remember each step of STOP."

5. Sing through the song and provide lyrics of the song for the children to sing along.
6. Present motions to the children to pair with the steps of the STOP skill:
   - Stop: hold out hand in front of you
   - Take a step back: take a step backward
   - Observe: hold hand over your eyes as if looking in the distance
   - Pick a healthy choice: hold your hand in front of you and make a motion like you are picking something out of the air.
7. Invite children to sing along and sing through again pairing the motions with the words.
8. Discussion questions:
   - Can you name the four steps of the STOP skill?
   - Can you remember a time where you used the STOP skill and made a healthy choice when angry?
   - What other emotions might you have where it can be good to stop and think before acting?
   - How can you observe? (For example, with eyes, ears, smell, touch.)

Stop Skill (to the tune of "Santa Claus is Coming to Town")

A
I want to act right
   D
when my emotions are high.
A
Think things through
 D
I'm telling you why:
A   E   A
The STOP skill can help me to make a healthy choice.

A
Before I react
D
I think of my goal;
A   D
My wise mind can stay in control.
A   E   A
The STOP skill can help me to make a healthy choice.

D
When I'm feeling _____
D
And want to act on my urges.
B7   E
I stop and take a step back
B7   E
Observe, then pick a healthy choice!

A
First I stop
 D
Then I take a step back.
A
Next I observe
 D
and pick a healthy choice.
A   E   A
The STOP skill can help me to make a healthy choice

Modifications for higher developmental level
MATERIALS NEEDED

- Visual of a STOP sign
- STOP written out with each step of the STOP skill after each letter
  - Stop
  - Take a Step Back
  - Observe
  - Proceed Mindfully
- Lyrics of the STOP skill song (included in the earlier lesson overview)

LESSON OVERVIEW

1. Show a stop sign and ask children if they know what it is.
2. State: "The STOP skill can help us to pause before acting so we can make a healthy choice."
3. Name the four steps of the STOP skill (pair with the letters of the word if appropriate for the children):
   - Stop

- Take a step back
- Observe
- Pick a healthy choice

4. State: "Today we will learn a song so we can remember each step of STOP."
5. Sing through the song and provide lyrics of the song for the children to sing along.
6. Present motions to the children to pair with the steps of the STOP skill:
   - Stop: hold out hand in front of you
   - Take a step back: take a step backward
   - Observe: hold hand over your eyes as if looking in the distance
   - Pick a healthy choice: hold your hand in front of you and make a motion like you are picking something out of the air.
7. Invite children to sing along and sing through again pairing the motions with the words.
8. Encourage the class to make a list of emotions they could put in the verse of the song.
9. Discussion questions:
   - Can you name the four steps of the STOP skill?
   - Can you remember a time where you used the STOP skill and made a healthy choice when angry?
   - What other emotions might you have where it can be good to stop and think before acting?
   - How can you observe? (For example, with eyes, ears, smell, touch.)

✿ "SHAKE DON'T SHOUT"

Module: Distress Tolerance

Skill addressed
STOP

Summary
The main goal of this activity is to teach the STOP skill, focusing on the first two steps while pairing it with movement and a familiar tune.

Materials needed

- Recording of "Twist and Shout" by The Beatles—if able, use an instrumental version—and means to play the song
- Maracas or shakers

Lesson preparation

- Cue audio
- Write on the board

  Stop
  Take a step back
  Observe
  Pick a healthy choice*

*Please note—This is a concrete adaptation from the typical *Proceed Mindfully*, which can be an abstract and more difficult concept for younger children.

Lesson overview

1. Review the STOP skill

   Stop
   Take a step back
   Observe
   Pick a healthy choice

2. Pass out maracas or shakers. Tell the students they will practice stopping four times. Ask students to practice Stop and Take a step back with the music. Play the maracas with the music as they walk around the room. Each time it stops—Stop and Take a step back.
3. Ask the students to observe their breathing and notice the quiet.

Modifications for higher developmental level

1. Review the STOP skill

   Stop
   Take a step back
   Observe
   Pick a healthy choice

2. Pass out maracas or shakers. Tell the students they will practice stopping four times. Ask students to practice Stop and Take a step back with the music. Play the maracas with the music as they walk around the room. Each time it stops—Stop and Take a step back.
3. Ask the students to observe their breathing and notice the quiet.
4. Now teach new words to the song:

   When I start to feel my urges (feel my urges)
   I remember stop! (Remember Stop)
   Come on, Come on, Come on, Come on, baby, now (come on baby)
   Stop and Freeze (Stop and Freeze)
   My emotions may try to take over (take over)
   I can stay in control (stay in control)
   I won't move a muscle (move a muscle)
   I just STOP (Remember Stop)

5. Repeat activity and this time have the students sing the chorus with the song and shake the maracas when they aren't singing.

FAVORITES

Module: Distress Tolerance

Skill addressed
Wise Mind "ACCEPTS" Activities

Summary
The main goal of this intervention is for students to identify five activities that they enjoy.

Materials needed

* Recording of a song that highlights things we love and/or enjoy (e.g. "My Favorite Things" from *The Sound of Music*; "I Love the Mountains"—folk song) and the means to play the audio
* Lyrics from the chosen song for songwriting
* Paper
* Markers, crayons, colored pencils

Lesson preparation

* Cue audio
* Have the lyrics to the chosen song visible for the students to see

Lesson overview

1. Introduce the idea of doing an activity to distract us when we feel upset. Explain: "Sometimes when we are having big emotions, it can be helpful to distract ourselves by doing something that we enjoy. It can be hard to think of those things in the moment when we are feeling upset or angry. That's why it can be helpful to think ahead and make a list of things we enjoy doing and could do in a future difficult moment."
2. Invite students to listen to the chosen song. Invite students to listen to what the person in the song liked or liked doing.
3. Have students raise their hand and share what they heard.
4. Pass out paper and writing/drawing materials to students.
5. Invite students to draw or write about five activities that they like doing.

(Optional: play song again or play music without lyrics in the background to help provide structure and timing to activity.)

6. Invite students to share some of their favorite activities.
7. Discussion questions:
    - Did you think or hear of any new activity that you might find fun?
    - Did any of your friend's activities sound like something you would be able to do?
    - If you are feeling a big emotion, what is one activity that you could do to help distract yourself for a time?
    - Have you ever used one of these activities to distract yourself before?

Modifications for higher developmental level

1. Introduce the idea of doing an activity to distract us when we feel upset. Explain: "Sometimes when we are having big emotions, it can be helpful to distract ourselves by doing something that we enjoy. It can be hard to think of those things in the moment when we are feeling upset or angry. That's why it can be helpful to think ahead and make a list of things we enjoy doing and could do in a future difficult moment."
2. Invite students to listen to the chosen song. Invite students to listen to what the person in the song liked or liked doing.
3. Have students raise their hand and share what they heard.
4. Use the lyrics from the chosen song and invite students to rewrite the lyrics (or fill in the blanks) with their own activities and things that they like. (Example: "_____ and _____, these are a few of my favorite things.")
5. Invite students to share with peers or in small groups, then proceed with discussion questions.
6. Discussion questions:
    - Did you think or hear of any new activity that you might find fun?
    - Did any of your friend's activities sound like something you would be able to do?
    - If you are feeling a big emotion, what is one activity that you could do to help distract yourself for a time?
    - Have you ever used one of these activities to distract yourself before?

❀ HELP ONE ANOTHER

Module: Distress Tolerance

Skill addressed
Wise Mind "ACCEPTS": Contributing

Summary
The main goal of this activity is to build tolerance to distress by helping others. In this intervention, students will identify three ways to help others.

Materials needed

- Recording of a song about helping friends and means to play the audio (e.g. "Leave the World Just a Little Bit Better" by Charlotte Diamond; "With a Little Help From My Friends" by the Beatles; "Count on Me" by Bruno Mars)
- Blank paper or coloring sheets with pictures of helping activities
- Markers, crayons, colored pencils

Lesson overview

1. Introduce activity: "Sometimes, when we are having big emotions, moving our focus away from ourselves and to someone else can distract us and help us get through tough times. This can look like helping another person, making something for a friend, or surprising someone with a drawing, note, or hug."
2. Invite students to share some ways that they could help a friend.
3. Introduce the chosen song: "Helping can make our world a little bit better and help us feel better too."
4. Invite children to draw a picture of three ways they can help a friend while listening to the song.
5. Play the chosen song.
6. When the song is over, ask students to share the ideas on their pictures.
7. Discussion questions:
   - What did you draw (or color) in your picture?
   - Have you ever helped in this way before?
   - What did you feel like when you helped?
   - Do you know how the other person felt when you helped?
   - What plan do you have to help someone today?

Modifications for higher developmental level
LESSON OVERVIEW

1. Introduce activity: "Sometimes, when we are having big, challenging emotions, moving our focus away from ourselves and to someone else can distract us and help us feel better—this is called "contributing." This can look like helping another person, making something for a friend, or surprising someone with a drawing, note, or hug."
2. Invite the students to share some ideas on how they can help someone in their lives and a way someone can help or has helped them.
3. Invite the students to write a thank you note to someone that has helped them this week while listening to the chosen song.
4. When the song is over, invite the students to share.
5. Discussion questions:
   - What does it feel like when you help someone or thank someone for what they have done?
   - Do you know how the other person felt when you helped?

✿ COLORS

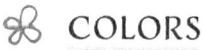

Module: Distress Tolerance

Skill addressed
Wise Mind "ACCEPTS": Comparison

Summary
The main goal of this activity is to observe a time someone felt sad and compare it to a time they did not.

Materials needed

- Recording of "The Day the Colors Went Away" by Shawny or a similar song related to both sadness and happiness and means to play the audio
- Lyrics of the song printed for children if desired
- Paper or coloring sheets
- A set of black, white, and gray crayons or markers
- A set of colorful markers

Lesson preparation

- Cue audio
- Pass out paper and black, white, and gray crayons or markers
- Have colorful crayons or markers ready to pass out to children

Lesson overview

1. Explain that "we all have days where we feel sad." Ask children to think of (or name if desired) a day or a moment when they felt sad in the past.
2. Pass out the set of black, white, and gray crayons or markers and paper. Say "sometimes our sad days can feel like they have no color."
3. Instruct children to draw a picture with the black, gray, and white colors while listening to the song.
4. Play the song while children color.
5. Share: "We also have days that are happy."
6. Pass out the colorful crayons or markers and another paper.
7. Instruct children to color a second picture using bright colors while you play the song a second time.

8. Discussion questions:
   - Can you think of a time you felt sad?
   - Do you think your feelings will last forever?
   - Do you think other people have days that feel like they have no color?
   - Can you think of a time when you felt happy?
9. Reinforce: "When we are having a difficult day or sad, it is helpful to compare it to a time we were happy to help remember we can get through challenges."

Modifications for higher developmental level
LESSON OVERVIEW

1. Explain that "we all have days where we feel sad." Ask children to think of (or name if desired) a day or a moment when they felt sad in the past.
2. Pass out the set of black, white, and gray crayons or markers and paper. Say "sometimes our sad days can feel like they have no color."
3. Instruct children to draw a picture with the black, gray, and white colors while listening to the song.
4. Play the song while children color.
5. Pass out the colorful crayons or markers and another paper. Say "after your sad day were you able to find color again and change from feeling sad to feeling happy?"
6. Instruct children to color a second picture using color while you play the song a second time.
7. Discussion questions:
   - When you are having a day with no color, what can help you find the color?
   - What can help you remember that feelings won't last forever?
8. Reinforce: "Comparing a time we felt happy when we are struggling can help us remember we are able to experience many different things. This can help us remember we can get through challenges."

✿ MUSIC TO SHIFT MY MOOD

Module: Distress Tolerance

Skill addressed

Wise Mind "ACCEPTS": with other EMOTIONS

Summary

The main goal of this activity is to distract one emotion through shifting our focus to other emotions through creating a list of three varying songs.

Materials needed

- Selected songs and means to play the audio (e.g. "Do the Next Right Thing" from Frozen 2; "Remember Me" from Coco; "You've Got a Friend in Me" from Toy Story; "A Dream is a Wish" from Cinderella; "Bare Necessities" from Jungle Book; and "Try Everything" from Zootopia)
- Paper or whiteboard

Lesson preparation

- Cue audio
- Prepare method of writing the list

Lesson overview

1. Explain: "We all experience emotions. Sometimes we have an emotion that we don't want to keep on feeling. We can do activities to help ourselves distract from the unwanted emotion by focusing on a different emotion."
2. Explain and prepare whiteboard or paper to write. "For example, an emotion we might not want to feel for a long time is sadness."
3. Write sad on top of the paper or board.
4. Ask children: "What is an emotion that we could feel other than sadness?"
5. Write down their answers.
6. Say: "We will listen to a few examples of songs. We can decide if some songs sound like the emotion of happiness or sadness (or include songs representing other emotions too, like fear and/or anger). We will choose three songs to create a playlist to distract from sadness."
7. Play examples of the following songs (or others you find that represent other emotions): "Do the Next Right Thing" from Frozen 2; "Remember

Me" from Coco; "You've Got a Friend in Me" from Toy Story; "A Dream is a Wish" from Cinderella; "Bare Necessities" from Jungle Book; and "Try Everything" from Zootopia.

8. Ask for children's opinion to choose the songs that represent sadness, happiness, and any other emotions.

9. Listen through the playlist of the three selected songs with the children.

10. Discussion questions:
   - Can you think of any other songs that represent happiness?
   - What other songs can you think of that represent other emotions, like anger or fear?

Modifications for higher developmental level
LESSON OVERVIEW

1. Explain: "We all experience emotions. Sometimes we have an emotion that we don't want to keep on feeling when it gets too big. We can do activities to help ourselves temporarily distract from one feeling to another."

2. Explain and prepare whiteboard or paper to write. "For example, an emotion we might not want to feel for a long time is sadness."

3. Write sad on top of the paper or board.

4. Ask children: "What is an emotion that would feel different from sadness?"

5. Add their answers to the paper.

6. Draw a line down from the word "sad" and write "happy" (and other emotions that they've listed).

7. Say: "We will listen to a few examples of songs. We can decide if some songs sound like the emotion happy, sad, or something else. We will choose three songs to create a playlist to distract from sadness to a different emotion."

8. Play examples of the following songs: "Do the Next Right Thing" from Frozen 2; "Remember Me" from Coco; "You've Got a Friend in Me" from Toy Story; "A Dream is a Wish" from Cinderella; "Bare Necessities" from Jungle Book; and "Try Everything" from Zootopia.

9. Ask for children's opinion to choose the songs that represent sadness, happiness, and any other emotions.

10. Listen through the playlist of three songs in order with the children.

11. Have the children add songs to each section of the playlist. Challenge them to create a playlist that has three songs for each section.

12. Discussion questions:
   - Can you think of any other songs that represent happiness?
   - What other songs can you think of that represent other emotions, like anger or fear?

❀ LOCK AND KEY

Module: Distress Tolerance

Skill addressed
Wise Mind "ACCEPTS": Pushing Away

Summary
The main goal of this activity is to practice pushing away a worry thought.

Materials needed

◆ Lyrics to the song (included in the lesson overview).
◆ A box for each child (e.g. empty tissue box, small cardboard boxes of various sizes, empty paper towel roll with one end taped over)
◆ Paper and writing utensil for children to write or draw a worry thought
◆ Printed picture of a lock or a drawn picture of a lock

Lesson preparation

◆ Write lyrics on a board for children to sing along
◆ Prepare materials to pass out to children

Lesson overview

1. Explain: "When we are having really big emotions, we can try to push these thoughts away to take a break from them."
2. Explain: "This doesn't mean we never come back to it, but we can put them aside until we feel calm".
3. Sing the lyrics of the song to the tune of the traditional nursery rhyme song "Rain, Rain, Go Away" (recording available at https://www.youtube.com/playlist?list=PL0jguhoPs0m6qrlhhTR7P4PPtz7wuicy1 or by scanning the QR code in the Appendix).

> *Worry thoughts, go away*
> *Put it in my box to stay.*
> *Write it down and lock it up.*
> *I can take a break today.*

4. Pass out the boxes and paper.
5. Invite children to think of a situation that may cause a big worry like a test they are nervous about. (Share other examples as needed.)
6. Invite children to write or draw the situation and place it in the box.
7. Sing the song and invite children to sing along as they place the paper in the box.
8. Offer children to cover the box with a lock. Explain: "It is locked for a break, but we still have the key, so when we are feeling calm we can come back to deal with the situation as needed."
9. Discussion questions:
    - Could you imagine putting your worry thoughts into the box?
    - Can you remember the song to sing next time you need to push a thought away?
    - What is easy about pushing away thoughts?
    - What is hard about pushing away thoughts?
    - What are other big emotions that you feel where you could use this song?

Modifications for higher developmental level

1. Explain: "When we are having really big emotions, we can try to push these thoughts away to take a break from them. This skill is not to avoid things we just don't want to do but is to be used when we have to calm down in the moment so we can move ahead."
2. Invite children to think of examples of the difference between things they just want to avoid versus things they need to push away (i.e. homework, studying, chores, listening to parents).
3. Lyrics can be chanted or rapped to a background beat found in a google search if more appropriate for the musical taste of the group and age.

Worry thoughts, go away
Put it in my box to stay.
Write it down and lock it up.
I can take a break today.

4. Pass out the boxes and paper.
5. Invite children to think of a situation that may cause them a big worry. (Share examples if needed.)
6. Invite children to write or draw the situation and place it in the box.

7. Sing, chant, or rap the song and invite children to sing along as they place the paper in the box.
8. Offer the option of covering the box with a lock. Explain: "It is locked for a break, but we still have the key, so when we are feeling calm we can come back to deal with the situation as needed."
9. Discussion questions:
   - Could you imagine putting your worry thoughts into the box?
   - Can you remember the song to sing next time you need to push a thought away?
   - What is easy about pushing away thoughts?
   - What is hard about pushing away thoughts?
   - What other challenging emotions do you feel; could you use this song to help?

✿ CHANGING OUR THOUGHTS

Module: Distress Tolerance

Skill addressed
Wise Mind "ACCEPTS": with other Thoughts

Summary
The main goal of this activity is to distract from stressful emotions through focusing on other thoughts like song lyrics.

Materials needed

◆ Lyrics to the songs "BINGO" (included in the lesson overview) and "Deep and Wide" (a traditional spiritual/folk song of Christian origin)

Lesson preparation

◆ Know the lyrics to the song you will present

Lesson overview

1. Explain: "When we feel big emotions we can help ourselves by changing our thoughts."
2. One way we can change our thoughts is by thinking about the words of a song.
3. Explain: "We can sing the song aloud or we can keep some of the words in our heads."
4. Sing the folk song "BINGO" and insert clapping for the letters in sequential order:

   There was a farmer had a dog,
   And Bingo was his name-o.
   B-I-N-G-O!
   B-I-N-G-O!
   B-I-N-G-O!
   And Bingo was his name-o!

   There was a farmer had a dog,
   And Bingo was his name-o.

(Clap)-I-N-G-O!

(Clap)-I-N-G-O!
(Clap)-I-N-G-O!
And Bingo was his name-o!

There was a farmer had a dog,
And Bingo was his name-o.
(Clap, clap)-N-G-O!
(Clap, clap)-N-G-O!
(Clap, clap)-N-G-O!
And Bingo was his name-o!

There was a farmer had a dog,
And Bingo was his name-o.

(Clap, clap, clap)-G-O!
(Clap, clap, clap)-G-O!
(Clap, clap, clap)-G-O!
And Bingo was his name-o!

There was a farmer had a dog,
And Bingo was his name-o.
(Clap, clap, clap, clap)-O!
(Clap, clap, clap, clap)-O!
(Clap, clap, clap, clap)-O!
And Bingo was his name-o!

There was a farmer had a dog,
And Bingo was his name-o.
(Clap, clap, clap, clap, clap)
(Clap, clap, clap, clap, clap)
(Clap, clap, clap, clap, clap)
And Bingo was his name-o!

5. The song "Deep and Wide" can also be utilized through using this format.

   a. First sing all the lyrics aloud.
   b. Sing again but insert a "hum" for the word "deep."
   c. Sing a third time but insert a "hum" for the word "deep" and "wide."

6. Discussion questions:
   - Did you hear the word in your head when you clapped or hummed?
   - Can you think of all the words in your head without saying them out loud?
   - Is there another song you know that you can think through all the words?
   - When you were singing the song or thinking of the lyrics, were you able to think about other things *or* were you distracted and focused on something fun?

Modifications for higher developmental levels

MATERIALS NEEDED

◆ Pick a popular song you can play a recording of

LESSON PREPARATION

◆ Prepare the lyrics of the song with one word missing from each line. For example, the traditional American song "Take Me Out to the Ball Game"

Take _____ out to the ball game
Take me _____ to the crowd
Buy me some _____ and crackerjack
I don't care if I _____ go back.

LESSON OVERVIEW

1. Explain: "When we feel big emotions sometimes it is hard for us to think of anything else. We can help ourselves by changing our thoughts. One way we can change our thoughts is thinking about the words of a song."
2. Pass out the prepared lyric sheet and ask students to get out a pencil.
3. Instruct the students to listen to the song and fill in the blanks with the correct word.
4. Discussion questions:
   - When you were filling in the words, what were you thinking of?
   - As you were distracted by the song and getting the correct word, do you think it would make it harder to be focused on other stressful things or emotions?

✿ SHOCKING SENSES

Module: Distress Tolerance

Skill addressed
Wise Mind ACCEPTS: Senses

Summary
The main goal of this activity is for children to use a song to be mindful of intense or shocking sensations that can distract them during a crisis situation.

Materials needed

- A recorded song that children may find irritating over time, for example a jingle played over and over like the "Slinky" jingle by Julie Branchard, or a theme song like "Baby Shark" by Pinkfong, and means to play the audio
- Items that can create a shocking sensation: ice pack, sour candy, a candle with a strong scent

Lesson preparation

- Have several items listed in lesson materials ready to share with the students

Lesson overview

1. Ask: "Who can tell me the five senses?" Write on the board: Sight, sound, touch, smell, and taste.
2. Explain: "We can learn to use our senses to distract us when upset through finding ways to use our senses to 'shock' us."
3. Pass out the sour candies.
4. Start playing the "irritating jingle."
5. Ask: "Does that song/jingle annoy you? Let's see if we can distract it away. Put the sour candy in your mouth. Now what has your attention?"
6. "Let's try it again."
7. Play the jingle again. Ask the students to put a really cold ice pack on their face when the jingle starts.
8. Play the jingle again. This time smell an unlit scented candle.
9. Discussion questions:
   - What item helped distract you best?

- What are other items that you could use to distract with your senses?

Modifications for higher developmental level

1. Ask: "Who can tell me the five senses?" Write on the board: Sight, sound, touch, smell, and taste.
2. Explain: "We can learn to use our senses to distract us when upset through finding ways to use our senses to 'shock' us."
3. Pass out the sour candies.
4. Start playing the "irritating jingle."
5. Ask: "Does that song/jingle annoy you? Let's see if we can distract it away. Put the sour candy in your mouth. Now what has your attention?"
6. "Let's try it again."
7. Play the jingle again. Ask the students to put a really cold ice pack on their face when the jingle starts.
8. Play the jingle again. This time smell an unlit scented candle.
9. Have the students create an index card of other items that might be shocking sensations (e.g. loud music, spicy food, sandpaper). Ask the students to share their ideas.
10. Discussion questions:
    - What items helped distract you best?
    - What items could you keep with you that could help distract you through using sensations that could shock you in the moment?

✿ CREATE YOUR WORLD

Module: Distress Tolerance

Skill addressed
IMPROVE the Moment: Imagery

Summary
The main goal of this activity is to imagine a safe place that is relaxing and practice using imagery to improve a difficult moment.

Materials needed

- A song like "What a Wonderful World" by Louis Armstong and means to play the audio
- Paper
- Drawing materials
- Glue/scissors
- Picture examples of beautiful places

Lesson overview

1. Explain: "When we feel strong or uncomfortable emotions it can help us to imagine a beautiful, safe place that we can picture in our minds for a short time. Imagining ourselves in a safe place where we make healthy and safe choices can help us feel relaxed and ready to face our current moment."
2. Continue: "It is important to practice picturing this wonderful world when we are calm so that we are ready to imagine it if we feel big emotions."
3. Invite students to listen to a song like "What a Wonderful World."
4. Invite students to close their eyes if they are comfortable and think about what a "wonderful world" looks like to them.
5. Show students a variety of pictures of beautiful places.
6. Ask students to choose pictures they like to make a collage by gluing on a larger piece of paper.
7. Play the song again and invite children to create a picture of what it would look like in their "wonderful world."
8. Discussion questions:
   - Can you share something that you pictured in your "wonderful world"?

- If you close your eyes, can you see even more details than the collage of your "wonderful world"?
- Can you imagine yourself calm and safe, making healthy choices in your world?
- What other emotions do you feel there?
- What was easy about imagining a "wonderful world"?
- Was there anything hard about imagining it?

Modifications for higher developmental level
LESSON OVERVIEW

1. Explain: "When we feel strong or uncomfortable emotions it can help us to imagine a beautiful, safe place that we can picture in our minds for a short time. Imagining ourselves in a safe place where we make healthy and safe choices can help us feel relaxed and ready to face our current moment."
2. Continue: "It is important to practice picturing this wonderful world when we are calm so that we are ready to imagine it if we feel big emotions."
3. Invite students to listen to a song like "What a Wonderful World."
4. After listening to the song once, pass out art materials.
5. Play the song again and invite children to draw a picture of what it would look like in their "wonderful world."
6. Discussion questions:
   - Can you share something that you pictured in your "wonderful world"?
   - If you close your eyes, can you see even more details than your drawing of your "wonderful world"?
   - Can you imagine yourself calm and safe, making healthy choices in your world?
   - What other emotions do you feel there?
   - What was easy about imagining a "wonderful world"?
   - Was there anything hard about imagining it?

✿ RAINY DAYS

Module: Distress Tolerance

Skill addressed
IMPROVE the Moment: Meaning

Summary
The main goal of this activity is to practice finding hope and meaning in difficult challenges.

Materials needed

- A piece of paper with an outline of a cloud drawn on
- Words of chant "Rain, Rain Go Away Come Back Another Day"

Lesson preparation

- Write the words of the chant "Rain, Rain Go Away Come Back Another Day" on the whiteboard

Lesson overview

1. Teach the chant to the children:

   Rain, Rain Go Away
   Come Back Another Day

2. Ask the students to identify when they do not like the rain (e.g. days when they would like to play outside; a day they are supposed to go camping).
3. Have them chant "Rain, Rain Go Away" and have children take turns standing up and sharing a day they would not like it to rain.
4. Now ask the children to share why the rain is important (e.g. drinking water, helping flowers grow).
5. Have them change the chant to "Rain, Rain Come Today" and have children take turns standing and sharing a reason the rain is important.
6. Share the skill: "Today we found meaning in something that we don't always like. Sometimes it is hard to find hope in challenges, but it can help us deal with hard days."

7. Discussion questions:
    - Can you think of a time when you were glad for the rain?
    - Can you think of a time when something that seemed to start bad ended up good? For example, "the coach wouldn't let me pitch for the game, but I ended up catching a ball at second base"; "I didn't get the doll I wanted for my birthday, but I got a game I really like playing."

Modifications for higher developmental level

1. Teach the chant to the children:

    Rain, Rain Go Away
    Come Back Another Day

2. Pass out the piece of paper with an outline of a cloud drawn on. Ask the students to identify when they do not like the rain (e.g. days when they would like to play outside; a day they are supposed to go camping).
3. Have them chant "Rain, Rain Go Away" and have children take turns standing up and sharing a day they would not like it to rain.
4. Now ask the children to share why the rain is important (e.g. drinking water, helping flowers grow).
5. Have them change the chant to "Rain, Rain Come Today" and have children take turns standing and sharing a reason the rain is important.
6. Share the skill: "Today we found meaning in something that we don't always like. Sometimes it is hard to find the good in bad things, but it can help us deal with hard days."
7. Discussion questions:
    - Can you think of a time when you were glad for the rain?
    - Can you think of a time when something that seemed to start bad ended up good? For example, "the coach wouldn't let me pitch for the game, but I ended up catching a ball at second base"; "I didn't get the doll I wanted for my birthday, but I got a game I really like playing."
8. Have each student identify one challenge they have or have had and list it inside the cloud on their worksheet. Then have each student write on their sheet one hopeful or positive thing that happened while they were going through that challenge or after the challenge ended. For example, inside my circle "I was scared I had to have my tonsils out." Outside my circle "I was allowed to eat popsicles and I don't get sore throats as many times as I used to." Have the students share their experiences and do the chant in between each student sharing.

❀ REFLECTIONS

Module: Distress Tolerance

Skill addressed
IMPROVE the Moment: Prayer

Summary
The main goal of this activity is to practice reflecting on things we are grateful for when we struggle; and prayer helps us connect with someone/thing outside of ourselves.

Materials needed

◆ Nature music and the means to play it in the background
◆ Whiteboard
◆ Paper, crayons, pencils

Lesson overview

1. Explain: "When we are having a difficult day, one thing that can help us is to reflect on things that we are grateful for. Reflective thought is a type of prayer." (Feel free to re-phrase the word "prayer" to "inner reflection" or something to that effect if there is any concern about the use of this language.)
2. Put soft nature music on in the background and ask each student to draw or write down three things they are grateful (thankful) for.
3. Have students share at least one thing they drew or wrote down and make a list on the whiteboard.
4. Create a classroom "Gratitude Prayer" or "Gratitude Reflection":

   We are grateful for friends.
   We are grateful for our pets.
   We are grateful for the sun.

5. Discussion questions:
   ▪ How can repeating this help us when we are mad or sad?

Modifications for higher developmental level

1. Explain: "When we are having a difficult day, one thing that can help us is to reflect on things that we are grateful for. Reflective thought is a type of prayer." (Feel free to re-phrase the word "prayer" to "inner reflection" or something to that effect if there is any concern about the use of this language.)
2. Put soft nature music on in the background and ask each student to draw or write down three things they are grateful (thankful) for.
3. Have students write out a "Gratitude Prayer" or "Gratitude Reflection":

   I am grateful for _____.
   I am grateful for _____.
   I am grateful for _____.

4. With the soft music still playing, have the children read their prayer/reflection for the class.
5. Discussion questions:
   - How can repeating this help us when we are upset?
   - Why is it helpful to reflect on items we are grateful for?
   - Do you have words (or prayers) that you recite that help you feel better?

❀ HOW I RELAX

Module: Distress Tolerance

Skill addressed
IMPROVE the Moment: Relaxing Actions

Summary
The main goal of this activity is to identify ways to relax.

Materials needed

- The song "When I Breathe" by Stephanie Leavell or another song that is slow and calming and means to play the audio
- Whiteboard or paper to write ideas of relaxing activities

Lesson overview

1. Explain: "When we have big emotions our body can feel tight and tense."
2. Offer an example and invite children to tighten their bodies.
3. Explain: "We can find activities that are relaxing to us to help our bodies feel loose, relaxed, and calm."
4. Explain: "After we listen to this song we can think of activities that might be relaxing to use."
5. Invite children to close their eyes and breathe with the song if desired.
6. Play the song "When I Breathe" by Stephanie Leavell or another calming song.
7. After the song, offer a pause of a time for silence for children to feel the experience of relaxation.
8. When appropriate, invite children to share an activity they find relaxing and write ideas on the board. Examples could include going on a walk outside, listening to music, petting a cat, getting a hug, coloring, reading a book.
9. If desired, replace the phrase "when I breathe" from the song with "when I _____" using an example shared by children.
10. Discussion questions:
    - Did you feel your body relax when you listened to the song?
    - Have you ever used one of these activities to relax before?
    - Can you show me a tense body?

- Can you show me a relaxed body?
- Can you think of a time you might need to use a relaxing activity?

Modifications for higher developmental level

1. Ask the students to identify ways their bodies and minds react when they are in stressful situations.
2. Ask if anyone has ever done relaxing things to calm down.
3. Have the students write two to four sentences to fill in different relaxation activities "when I _____" as you play "When I Breathe" or another calming song.
4. Have the students share their lines and compile a list of relaxing activities on the board. (They can share the line they wrote as the song is quietly playing in the background.)
5. Play the song one more time, and have the students do some simple stretching to practice a relaxing activity.
6. Discussion questions:
   - What other things do you notice in your body when you are upset?
   - What do you notice in your body when you are relaxed?
   - When is it important to practice relaxing?
   - How can you practice relaxing today?

✿ ONE MOMENT PLEASE

Module: Distress Tolerance

Skill addressed
IMPROVE the Moment: One Thing in the Moment

Summary
The main goal of this activity is to practice doing one thing in the moment (one thing at a time).

Materials needed

◆ A recorded song like "Big Love, Small Moments" by JJ Heller or another song with a steady beat and means to play the audio

Lesson overview

1. Practicing one thing at a time is called living "one-mindfully." When we feel big emotions it can help to slow down and focus on one thing.
2. Offer examples to the students of when it is helpful to do one thing at a time:
   - I feel like I have to do all of my chores at the same time; I can focus on just one right now.
   - I have three homework assignments; I can pick just one of them to focus on and do it first.
   - I have too many things to do to take care of the dog; I can feed him, and then later take him for a walk.
3. "Now we're going to practice doing one thing. And that one thing is tapping. We will be tapping along to a song. The start of the song is like a heartbeat. Your heart beats one beat at a time. We will make that heartbeat sound by tapping with one hand on our lap."
4. "While you tap, notice if your mind wanders to something else and bring it back to tapping."
5. Play the song "Big Love, Small Moments" by JJ Heller. Play a minimum of 30 seconds of the song and model tapping with one hand.
6. Discussion questions:
   - Could you do the one thing (tapping your hand) through the song?

- Did you notice your mind wandering at any point? Could you bring it back to tapping?
- What was easy about doing one thing at a time?
- What was hard about doing one thing at a time?
- What helped when you did one thing at a time?
- What got in the way when you did one thing at a time?

Modifications for higher developmental level

1. Practicing one thing at a time is called living "one-mindfully." When we feel big emotions it can help to slow down and focus on one thing.
2. Offer examples to the students of when it is helpful to do one thing at a time:
   - I feel like I have to do all of my chores at the same time; I can focus on just one right now.
   - I have three homework assignments; I can pick just one of them to focus on and do it first.
   - I have too many things to do to take care of the dog; I can feed him, and then later take him for a walk.
3. Ask students to share examples.
4. "Now we're going to practice doing one thing. And that one thing is tapping. We will be tapping along to a song. The start of the song is like a heartbeat. Your heart beats one beat at a time. We will make that heartbeat sound by tapping with one hand on our lap."
5. "While you tap, notice if your mind wanders to something else and bring it back to tapping."
6. Play the song "Big Love, Small Moments" by JJ Heller. Play a minimum of one minute of the song and model tapping with one hand.
7. Discussion questions:
   - Have you ever had an experience where you felt overwhelmed by trying to solve more than one problem? How could you use the skill "one thing at a time"?
   - What would you do if this happens again?
   - Play an additional one minute of the song and invite children to listen to the lyrics where it says "small moments."
   - Invite students to pause and notice this moment and take it in. Ask what they notice.

VACATION SPOTS

Module: Distress Tolerance

Skill addressed

IMPROVE the Moment: "a brief" Vacation

Summary

The main goal of this activity is to use one's imagination to create an enjoyable vacation spot.

Materials needed

- Recording of a song, such as "Ukulele in a Snowstorm" by the Okee Dokee Brothers, for the included discussion questions and means to play the audio
- Optional: pictures of different ideas of vacation spots and/or paper and way for students to draw

Lesson overview

1. Explain: "In tough moments, it can be helpful to take a mini-vacation. Mini-vacations can help us breathe easier, rest our brain, and think more positively."
2. Continue: "For example, if it's snowing and you don't like the snow, you could imagine being in the sun. In this song, they are in a place with a lot of snow and they imagine a vacation in Hawaii when they were sad about the snow."
3. Listen to the song.
4. Have the students imagine their favorite vacation spot. Share examples of the pictures if desired.
5. Invite the students to draw a picture of their vacation spot.
6. Play the song as they draw.
7. Discussion questions:
    - Did you picture a relaxing vacation spot?
    - Can you share what it looked like?
    - Have you ever been in snow and wished for a warm day on the beach?
    - What was it like to imagine a vacation?

- If you are feeling big emotions, what kind of vacation spot could you imagine?

Modifications for higher developmental level
MATERIALS NEEDED

- Magazines, glue, scissors, paper, markers, colored pencils, crayons
- Search for "Lo-fi music for the classroom" or any lo-fi music that can be found on YouTube or your preferred music app

LESSON OVERVIEW

1. Explain to the students that we can use the IMPROVE skill when we are upset by picturing a place we want to visit, have visited, or even a made-up place where we feel safe. When we do this we are using the "V" in IMPROVE to take a mini-vacation.
2. Instruct the students to go through the pictures in the magazines or other pictures provided and find a few that could represent their "mini-vacation spot."
3. Have them glue their chosen pictures on a piece of paper.
4. While the students are creating their collages, play any lo-fi song or mix.
5. After the students have completed their collages, ask them to go on a journey to their vacation spot as they imagine being there.
6. Start the music again or pick a different lo-fi song geared more towards relaxation.
7. Discussion questions:
   - Were you able to find or draw your vacation spot?
   - How easy was it to take a "mini-vacation" and visualize your vacation spot?
   - What was hard about this activity?
   - What changed or is different after this activity?

❀ I KNOW I CAN

Module: Distress Tolerance

Skill addressed
IMPROVE the Moment: Encouragement

Summary
The main goal of this activity is to identify words that encourage us and make encouraging reminders to use during challenges.

Materials needed

+ Encouraging children's song (e.g. "What I Am, A Sesame Street Song" by Will.I.Am, "I Can" by Nas, "Try Everything" by Shakira, "I Can Do Things" by Stephanie Leavell) and means to play the audio
+ Whiteboard and markers
+ Cardstock cut into rectangles for bookmarks
+ Drawing materials

Lesson preparation

+ Cue audio
+ Find or make worksheets with encouraging words on
+ Examples of words to use: smart, brave, strong, thoughtful, helpful, special

Lesson overview

1. Hold up papers with encouraging words on for the students.
2. Ask the students to say "I am" and then hold up each word and ask the student to say it (e.g. "I am smart"; "I am brave") until they have read them all.
3. Ask each student to pick one paper.
4. Ask the students to color their favorite one while you all listen to one of the songs listed.
5. Post the pictures where the students can see them.
6. Discussion questions:
   - What feelings happen when you look at your pictures?

- What other words give you encouragement?

Modifications for higher developmental level

1. Listen to the song and have children list positive words or phrases they hear (e.g. "dream"; "never gonna stop"; "keep getting stronger"; "smart"; "special") and write them on the board.
2. Ask students to write their favorite words on their cardboard bookmark.
3. Say, "When we are having a tough day, time, or moment, we all need reminders that we are special, strong, smart, and kind. Keep your bookmark with you and use it when you need this reminder."

✿ IT IS ME

Module: Distress Tolerance

Skill addressed
IMPROVE the Moment: "Self" Encouragement

Summary
The main goal of this activity is to encourage one's self through a difficult moment by creating a list of positives about one's self.

Materials needed

- Song like "I Love My Body" by Mother Moon or "Head, Shoulders, Knees, and Toes" that references parts of the body and means to play the audio
- Large mirror

Lesson overview

1. Have students stand in front of a big mirror, then play/sing this song.
2. Direct the student to point to each body part as it's sung in the song.
3. During the chorus pause the music and engage the students in a call and response:

   Teacher: "Who is that?"
   Students (stand up and shout): "It's me!"
   Teacher: "And I'm looking…"
   Students: "Good as good can be."
   Teacher: "So what do I say? I tell myself…"
   Students: "I love me every day."

4. Discussion questions:
   - What are some other positive things that you can tell yourself about you?
   - What do you like about yourself?
   - What makes you special?

Modifications for higher developmental level

1. Have students stand in front of a big mirror as you play/sing the song.

2. Ask the children: "Is it easy to see positives in ourselves? It is important for us to practice saying positive things about ourselves. Let's practice. Stand up with me:

    Teacher: "Who is that?"
    Students (stand up and shout): "It's me!"
    Teacher: "And I'm looking…"
    Students: "Good as good can be."
    Teacher: "So what do I say? I tell myself…"
    Students: "I love me every day."

3. Discussion questions:
    -   What are some other positive things you can tell yourself about you?
    -   What do you like about yourself?
    -   What makes you special?
    -   Why is it important to practice looking at ourselves and saying positive things?

✿ TEA POT TIP

Module: Distress Tolerance

Skill addressed
TIP

Summary
The main goal of this activity is to learn ways we can regulate our body's physiological response to distress when experiencing very big emotions.

Materials needed

- Music with a strong beat to move along with and means to play the audio
- Relaxation music like ocean waves
- Cooler with ice packs

Lesson overview

1. TIP can be taught in 1 large lesson or in any combination of the 4 exercises listed below.
2. Sing and do the actions to the nursery rhyme:

   I'm a little tea pot
   short and stout
   TIP me over and
   pour me out

3. Discuss: "What happens when a tea pot gets hot? What happens when you have a strong emotion (e.g. hot, tense, restless)? When we get hot, there are ways to help ourselves with our body."
4. Teach T for Temperature:
   - Do you ever get hot when you are upset?
   - What are ways we cool down?
   - Have ice packs in a cooler and teach children how they can access them when they need one in the future (e.g. ask teacher, go to nurse, etc.).
5. Teach I for Intense Exercise:
   - "Let's blow off some steam through a little exercise."

- Put on a song with a strong beat and have them choose between moves—arm circles, marching in place, jumping jacks, squatting up and down.

6. Teach P for Paced Breathing:
   - "Now let's practice a special way to breathe that helps us calm down using counts of two and four—Breathe in, 2,3,4. Hold, 2. Breathe out, 2,3,4." Repeat four times.

7. Teach P for Paired Muscle Relaxation:
   - "Now let's relax our muscles" (put on the relaxing music).
   - Sit in your chair with your feet on the floor—read the following script to the students. (Remind your students that if a muscle hurts to stop and join in when they can.)

> "Rest your eyes looking down at your feet
> Breathe in and out
> Close your eyes nice and tight—squeeze them shut
> (Silently pause for a count to 4)
> Now rest your eyes
> Open your jaw nice and wide
> (Silently pause for a count to 4)
> Now rest your lips
> Lift your shoulders up to your ears
> (Silently pause for a count to 4)
> Let them drop
> Tighten your hands like you are squeezing an orange
> (Silently pause for a count to 4)
> Rest your hands in your lap
> Push your feet into the floor like you are pushing them into mud
> (Silently pause for a count to 4)
> Now take a breath and rest your whole body."

Modifications for higher developmental level

♦ Depending on your class, one can skip the tea pot chant, but continue to reference what happens to a tea pot when it gets hot.

GRIZZLY BEAR GRUMP

Module: Distress Tolerance

Skill addressed

TIP—Intense exercise

Summary

The main goal of this activity is to move our bodies when we feel intense emotion.

Materials needed

- A recording of "Grizzly Bear Grump" by Stephanie Leavell and means to play the audio (recording available at https://youtu.be/jfetTpH7YIA)
- Screen for watching video (or can be done with just the song, and no video)
- 3x5 cards or pieces of paper for students to write down ideas
- Markers, crayons, colored pencils

Lesson preparation

- Please visit Stephanie Leavell's website: www.musicforkiddos.com/blog/a-song-about-feeling-mad-and-using-movement-for-self-regulation-grizzly-bear-grump
- Cue audio or video
- Have the lyrics of Grizzly Bear Grump up on screen or board (see lyrics at the end of this exercise, you can also download a copy to print from www.jkp.com/catalogue/book/9781805013211). Note: this activity is most effective when paired with the video

Lesson overview

1. Explain: "Sometimes we feel mad—who can show me their angry face? Sometimes we feel sad—who can show me their sad face? Sometimes we feel scared—who can show me their scared or worried face? When we feel these feelings, sometimes we need a way to let those feelings out in a healthy way. We are going to be a grizzly bear today who is feeling pretty grumpy. Let's see what grizzly bears do when they are feeling mad."

2. This activity will be best utilized with the audio and video shared. Show the video of Grizzly Bear Grump and invite students to move along with the bear.

3. Discussion questions:
   - What did the grizzly bear do to help their grumps? (Stomp, squeeze arms, etc.)
   - What are some other safe ways that you like to move when you are feeling angry? Frustrated? Scared? Take suggestions and invite all the students to try those suggestions (dance, run in place, jumping jacks, etc.).

Modifications for higher developmental level

1. Have students write down an emotion and a corresponding exercise they can use to help release the emotion. (E.g. When I feel mad I can stomp my feet or run fast.)

2. Have students create ideas for other animals/creatures (e.g. Sad Sally the Snake) to express different emotions and how they would move/what would calm them down. It's important to note though that the aim of this skill is to increase heart rate with physical activity, which then induces physical relaxation afterwards, so it does not matter what emotion is being experienced, the movements would need to be of high intensity.

3. This could also be turned into an art project.

4. Do a group rewrite of the lyrics and move to it with the new lyrics and movements.

5. Example:

   I am a _____ (animal),
   I feel really _____ (emotion),
   and when I feel bad I make sure to move my body.
   I can _____ (movement),
   _____ (2nd movement),
   _____ (3rd movement),
   Stretch up and say _____ (sound).

6. Have students brainstorm other songs that talk about moving their body (e.g. "Better When I'm Dancing" by Meghan Trainor).

"Grizzly Bear Grump" by Stephanie Leavell

Hey, oooh
Hey, oooh

I'm a grizzly bear grump
I feel really mad
And when I feel bad
I make sure to move my body

I can stomp my feet
STOMP STOMP
Squeeze my arms
SQUEEZE SQUEEZE
Twist my shoulders
TWIST TWIST
Stretch up and say GRRR

I'm a grizzly bear grump
I feel really mad
And when I feel bad
I make sure to move my body

Hey, I'm starting to feel better
Hey, I'm starting to feel better

Oooh

❧ BREATHE

Module: Distress Tolerance

Skill addressed
TIP—Paced Breathing

Summary
The main goal of this activity is for children to learn and engage in a breathing strategy by pairing their breath to music.

Materials needed

- A recorded song to facilitate slow, regulated breathing and means to play the audio. Examples are as follows:
  - "The Aquarium" by Saint-Saëns
  - "The Swan" by Saint-Saëns
  - "Clair de Lune" by Claude Debussy
  - "Prelude in E Minor" by Frederic Chopin
  - "Moonlight Sonata (first movement)" by Ludwig van Beethoven
  - "Piano Concerto in F-sharp minor (second movement)" by Hans von Bronsart
  - "Gymnopedie No.1" by Erik Satie
- Hoberman sphere ball that expands out and in
- OR shapes—circle, square, rectangle, triangle (drawn on the board or printed)

Lesson preparation

- Cue audio
- Have shapes or sphere easily accessible

Lesson overview

1. Explain: "Today we will use music to slow down and learn how to take regulated breaths. Slow breaths can help us to calm our heartbeat and reduce our stress. It can help to have something to look at while we practice slowing our breath."

2. Choose one of the following breathing techniques to share with the students and breathe with the music:

    ■ **Cloud breathing**: Take a big deep breath in as if you are inhaling a big fluffy cloud. Allow the cloud to expand inside you. Now exhale through your mouth, releasing the cloud as you imagine it drifting away.

    ■ **Rainbow breathing**: Imagine painting a rainbow in the sky. Start with your arms at your side, and palms facing forwards. Now imagine creating the red layer of a rainbow, breathing in as your arms create an arch reaching up from your sides. Slowly bring your arms back down to your sides as you breathe out. Repeating this for each color of the rainbow...orange, yellow, green, blue, and purple.

    ■ **Belly breathing**: Close your mouth and take a slow, deep breath in through your nose. When you breathe in, you want your belly to fill with air and get bigger like a balloon. Blow all of the air out slowly as if you are blowing bubbles.

    ■ **Six-sided breathing**: Draw a hexagon on the board. Trace first side breathing in. Hold as you trace across the top. Breathe out as you trace the third side. Breathe in as you trace the fourth side. Hold as you trace along the bottom. Breathe out as you trace the sixth side.

    ■ **Trace shapes while breathing**. Use prepared visuals.
        – **Star breathing**: Take a breath in with a side and hold at the point. Breathe out the second side. Repeat four additional times tracing the entire star.
        – **Triangle breathing**: Starting at one corner, breathe in for three seconds as you trace the side. Hold for three seconds as you trace the second side. Breathe out for three as you trace the third side.
        – **Square breathing**: Start at the bottom right of the square, breathe in as you trace the side. Hold for four as you trace the top of the square. Breathe out as you trace the third side. Hold for four as you trace the bottom of the square.

    ■ Use a **Hoberman sphere** and expand it in and out. Have the children breathe in as it expands and breathe out as it moves in.

CALMING SENSES, BIG EMOTIONS

Module: Distress Tolerance

Skill addressed

Self-soothe

Summary

The main goal of this activity is to learn to use the five senses to calm ourselves when faced with stressful situations.

Materials needed

- Whiteboard with markers or smartboard

Lesson preparation

- On the whiteboard, or smartboard, have pictures of the five senses
- Above Sight have the number 5; Touch have the number 4; Hear have the number 3; Smell have the number 2; Taste have the number 1

Lesson overview

1. Explain: 'Sometimes, when we are feeling big emotions, like anger, fear, or sadness, we need a way to help ourselves feel better. We can use our senses to help us calm down." Have the students recite the five senses.
2. Use this chant to remind students of the five senses:

   My eyes can see, see, see
   My fingers touch, touch, touch
   My ears can hear, hear, hear
   My nose can smell smell smell
   My tongue can taste taste taste

3. Now sing the following song, to the tune of "If You're Happy and You Know It," to help students learn how to self-soothe with their senses.

   When you're feeling big emotions, SEE FIVE things, (point to eyes)
   When you're feeling big emotions, SEE FIVE things, (point to eyes)

When you're feeling big emotions, and feel you have the notion, to act on those emotions, SEE FIVE things. (point to eyes)

*Stop song to identify 5 things the students can see

When you're feeling big emotions, TOUCH FOUR things, (clap clap or snap snap)
When you're feeling big emotions, TOUCH FOUR things, (clap clap or snap snap)
When you're feeling big emotions, and feel you have the notion, to act on those emotions, TOUCH FOUR things. (clap clap or snap snap)

*Stop song to identify 4 things students can touch

When you're feeling big emotions, HEAR THREE things, (tap ears)
When you're feeling big emotions, HEAR THREE things, (tap ears)
When you're feeling big emotions, and feel you have the notion, to act on those emotions, HEAR THREE things. (tap ears)

*Stop song to identify 3 things students can hear

When you're feeling big emotions, SMELL TWO things, (tap nose)
When you're feeling big emotions, SMELL TWO things, (tap nose)
When you're feeling big emotions, and feel you have the notion, to act on those emotions, SMELL TWO things. (tap nose)

*Stop song to identify 2 things students can smell

When you're feeling big emotions, TASTE ONE thing, (click tongue)
When you're feeling big emotions, TASTE ONE thing, (click tongue)
When you're feeling big emotions, and feel you have the notion, to act on those emotions, TASTE ONE thing. (click tongue)

*Stop song to identify 1 thing the students can taste

4. Repeat the song as many times as wanted (without the pauses in between). The more repetition, the better.

Modifications for higher developmental levels

1. Turn the "Big Emotion" song lyrics into a rap or chant.
    - Prompt the students to help fill in the blanks with their own emotions
    - Challenge students to come up with many different words for their emotions (e.g. instead of angry or mad, use furious or frustrated)
    - At the end of the rap/chant (or at the end of every verse), have the students state the 5 things they can see, 4 things they can feel, 3 things they can hear, 2 things they can smell, and 1 thing they can taste.
2. Separate into small groups and have each group come up with a short dance/movement to add for their verse. How can the dance/movement reflect the emotion?

Big Emotion Chant

When you're feeling (emotion word), SEE FIVE things,
When you're feeling (same emotion), SEE FIVE things,
When you're feeling big emotions, and feel you have the notion, to act on those emotions, SEE FIVE things.

When you're feeling (new emotion word), TOUCH FOUR things,
When you're feeling (same emotion), TOUCH FOUR things,
When you're feeling big emotions, and feel you have the notion to act on those emotions, TOUCH FOUR things.

When you're feeling (new emotion word), HEAR THREE things,
When you're feeling (same emotion), HEAR THREE things,
When you're feeling big emotions, and feel you have the notion, to act on those emotions, HEAR THREE things.

When you're feeling (new emotion word), SMELL TWO things,
When you're feeling (same emotion), SMELL TWO things,
When you're feeling big emotions, and feel you have the notion to act on those emotions, SMELL TWO things.

When you're feeling (new emotion word), TASTE ONE thing,
When you're feeling (same emotion), TASTE ONE thing,
When you're feeling big emotions, and feel you have the notion to act on those emotions, TASTE ONE thing.

✿ PROS AND CONS

Module: Distress Tolerance

Skill addressed
Pros and Cons

Summary
The main goal of this activity is to learn to stop and think before acting, and to weigh the consequences of your actions.

Materials needed

- Pros and cons chant lyrics (included in Lesson preparation)
- Recordings available at https://www.youtube.com/playlist?list=PL0jguho Ps0m6qrlhhTR7P4PPtz7wuicy1 or by scanning the QR code in the Appendix

Lesson preparation

- There are several variations you can choose from for the lyrics. Select one, even though it may vary from the recording, and use the version of your choice.

Original lyrics:
Pros and cons
Pros and cons
Think about the consequences when I feel my urges
Think about the consequences when I feel my urges
Stop and think
Stop and think

Variation 1:
Pros and cons
Pros and cons
Think about the consequences of my actions
Think about the consequences of my actions
Stop and think
Stop and think

Variation 2:
Pros and cons
Pros and cons
Think about my choices before I take action
Think about my choices before I take action
Stop and think
Stop and think

Lesson overview

1. Listen to the recording to get the rhythm. Stop it before the movements are introduced (at about the one-minute mark).
2. Teach the chant line by line by having the students repeat after you.
3. Say the entire chant as a group several times over.
4. Watch the remainder of the video. Add movements.

Pros and Cons
Pros and Cons. (Stomp feet in rhythm with the words)
Think about the consequences when I feel my urges
Think about the consequences when I feel my urges
(Rub hands together in rhythm with the words)
Stop and think
Stop and think
(Stop, clap, point to head)

5. Discussion question:
   - Why is it helpful to think before acting?

Modifications for higher developmental level

1. Listen to the recording to get the rhythm. Stop it before the movements are introduced (at about the one-minute mark).
2. Teach the chant line by line by having the students repeat after you.
3. Say the entire chant as a group several times over.
4. Explain to the students that you will be dividing them into three groups. Play the audio recording of the chant done in a round so they can see what is coming: (available at https://www.youtube.com/playlist?list=P L0jguhoPs0m6qrlhhTR7P4PPtz7wuicy1 or by scanning the QR code in the Appendix).

5. Divide the group into three parts:
   a. Group one says pros and cons over and over.
   b. Then add group two saying think about the consequences line over and over
   c. Then add group three saying stop and think over and over
6. Discussion questions:
   - Why is it a good idea to think before acting?
   - Have you ever acted without thinking? If so, how did you feel? What happened?
   - Have you ever stopped yourself from doing something because you thought about the consequences first? Were you glad you did?

✿ THE ACCEPTANCE TREE

Module: Distress Tolerance

Skill addressed
Radical Acceptance

Summary
The main goal of this activity is to explore ways to accept changes outside of one's control.

Materials needed

- Recorded music and means to play it—recommended music for this activity is instrumental music with nature sounds in the background as the class explores their "tree"
- Paper and coloring materials

Lesson preparation

- Cue audio
- Distribute paper and coloring materials to each student

Lesson overview

1. Preface this activity with a definition of radical acceptance. Radical acceptance is about acknowledging things we cannot change. Acceptance does not mean approval or liking something, but learning to live with something (at least for the moment).
2. Just because you accept something doesn't mean you have to like it. For example: You get ice cream with nuts in it. You can accept that ice cream has nuts in it even though you don't like nuts.
3. Ask the children to draw a picture of a beautiful tree. Or provide an outline of a tree that they can color.
4. Begin the music and stop it after 3–5 minutes (whatever works best in your classroom).
5. Stop the music, and ask the children to pass their paper to the person next to them.

6. Ask the students to add to the other child's tree until the music stops (play music for two minutes).
7. Repeat 1–3 times.
8. Return the tree to the original student.
9. Ask: "Are you happy or sad with the changes made to your tree?"
10. State: "Sometimes we cannot stop things from happening to the things we love, but we can learn to be okay with the changes."
11. Discussion questions:
    - Are you able to accept that people made changes to your tree?
    - What is one thing added to your drawing you may not have thought of, but like in the end?
    - Are there things that were added that you don't like? Can you still be okay with it without liking it?

Modifications for higher developmental level
LESSON PREPARATION

- Distribute paper and coloring materials to each student
- Set up 5–10 stations that have a large piece of paper and coloring materials at the station. Number each station

Lesson overview

1. Preface this activity with a definition of radical acceptance—accepting something for what it is. Just because you accept something doesn't mean you have to like it.
2. Have the students evenly distributed at each station (if 20 students and 10 stations, 2 per station)
3. Play music.
4. Direct them to make an abstract scribble.
5. Stop the music. Instruct students to look at their scribble and ask them: "Can you see a picture in it? What picture do you see? Color in the picture you see."
6. Play music for 2 minutes while they color in the shape.
7. Stop the music and have students pick a new number out of a hat that tells them which station to go next.
8. At the new station, invite students to look at the scribble that's on the paper. Ask: "Can you see a picture in it? What picture do you see? Color in the picture you see."

9. Play the music while they color for 2 minutes.
10. Continue switching.
11. End with their original artwork.
12. Discussion questions:
    - Are you able to accept that people made changes to your work?
    - What is one thing added to your drawing you may not have thought of, but like in the end?
    - When you look at your picture now, was anything easy to accept that changed?
    - Was anything hard?

✺ TURN THE MIND

Module: Distress Tolerance

Skill addressed
Radical Acceptance: Turning the Mind

Summary
The main goal is to practice turning the mind and choosing to accept what is in the present moment.

Materials needed

- Recorded music and means to play the audio
- A chair for each child (or station for each participant)
- Items to use as a drum (e.g. yogurt or coffee containers, cups, or bowls); have one such instrument for half of the class
- Items that are not as easily used as drums/instruments (e.g. feathers, scarves, pencils, etc.) for the other half of the class

Lesson preparation

- Cue audio
- Have the words to the Turning the Mind chant written on a whiteboard or on a smartboard:

> *You get what you get, and you don't mind a bit!*
> *Steady Beat: (pat)   (pat)   (pat)   (pat)*
> *If there's something you don't like, Turn your mind, Turn Your Mind…*
> *(pat)   (pat)   (pat)   (pat)*
> *(Clap Clap Clap)*
> *Maybe Next Time!*
> *(hold hands open, palms up)*

- Set up a station or chair for each student in a circle formation. At each station or chair place one "drum" (yogurt containers or coffee container) or one lighter item (feathers or scarves, pencils, etc.). Make sure to mix it up, so the lighter item and the drums are alternating

Lesson overview

1. Explain: "Sometimes we get to do or play with what we are hoping for. Other times, we must work with what we are given. When that happens, we get to practice being flexible: "You get what you get and you don't mind a bit. If there's something you don't like, turn your mind, turn your mind. Say, maybe next time!""

2. Teach the students the "Turning the Mind" chant by using a steady beat (patting on legs) and repeating the chant until it feels like the students are comfortable and familiar with it.

3. Start a game similar to Musical Chairs:
   a. Students walk around the outside while chosen recorded music plays. When the music stops, students stop where they are and sit down at the station or chair closest to them.
   b. Students then use the drum or light item to accompany the chant.
   c. Have the students repeat the chant twice.
   d. Start the recorded music and play as many times as time allows!

4. Discussion questions:
   - How did it feel when you got the item you wanted?
   - How did your feelings change when you got an item you didn't want?
   - Were you able to find a way to use the items that were not drums?
   - Did it get easier over time to be flexible?
   - Did it help to know that you might have a chance next time?

Modifications for higher developmental level

1. Explain: "Sometimes we get to do or play with what we are hoping for. Other times, we must work with what we are given. When that happens, we get to practice being flexible: 'You get what you get, and you don't mind a bit. If there's something you don't like, turn your mind, turn your mind. Say, maybe next time!' Turning the mind means choosing to accept reality as it is in the moment. It takes practicing this skill many times to come to radical acceptance. If something feels unacceptable, turn the mind."

2. Teach the students the "Turning the Mind" chant by using a steady beat (patting on legs) and repeating the chant until it feels like the students are comfortable and familiar with it.

3. Start a game similar to Musical Chairs:
   a. Students walk around the outside while chosen recorded music plays.

When the music stops, students stop where they are and sit down at the station or chair closest to them.

b. Students then use the drum or light item to accompany the chant.

c. Have the students repeat the chant twice.

d. Start the recorded music and play as many times as time allows!

4. Discussion questions:

- How did it feel when you got the item you wanted?
- How did your feelings change when you got an item you didn't want?
- Were you able to find a way to use the items that were not drums?
- Did it get easier over time to be flexible?
- Did it help to know that you might have a chance next time?
- Have you had an experience in your life where something happened that was hard to accept?
- How did you Turn the Mind?
- How could you use Turn the Mind in the future when you encounter a situation that's hard to accept?

✿ WILLING TO TRY

Module: Distress Tolerance

Skill addressed
Radical Acceptance: Willingness and Willing Hands

Summary
The main goal of this exercise is to practice willingness through a "mirror dance" in which partners will accept the movements of their mirror and imitate them.

Materials needed

- A recorded song like "Try Everything" by Shakira that encourages doing something new and means to play the audio

Lesson overview

1. Explain that "sometimes things happen in our life that we don't really like; and, if we are **wilful**, we whine and complain and do things that may make the problem worse."
2. Explain: "A more helpful way to manage things we don't like is to choose **willingness**, we accept what happens and do what we need to do to get through the situation."
3. Continue: "An example of **wilfulness** might be that our teacher tells us to line up for art class. You want to finish building your Lego creation, and so you stay in your chair and refuse to leave. You complain about having to leave and argue with your teacher. Now you and your class are late to art. An example of **willingness** would be to accept that it is time to move on, even though you don't want to, and find time later in the day to come back to your Lego creation. Now you and your class get to participate in art for the entire time."
4. Prompt students to partner up or assign partners for each student.
5. Explain: "We can practice willingness by following the lead of a partner in a dance."
6. Invite students to pick a leader or assign a leader for the dance.
7. Invite students to make different movements by lifting arms up and down, in and out, around in circles, or any movements they choose.

8. Invite students to practice willingness by following their partner without complaining and responding to the movements as best as they can.

9. Play the song for students to practice willingness for 1 minute 25 seconds, then pause the music.

10. Explain: "An easy way to help ourselves feel more willing is to hold our hands out in front of us in an open position with our palms facing up. This is called **willing hands**."

11. Explain: "In this song we are going to practice willing hands every time we hear the words 'Try everything' in the chorus." (Or use any repeated lyric.)

12. Start the song, then pause at 1 minute 25 seconds (when the lyrics say "try everything") and invite students to practice "willing hands."

13. Play through the song a second time after prompting the students to switch the leader and follower. Remind them to listen to the cue for "willing hands."

14. Discussion questions:
    - Did you demonstrate willingness while following your partner?
    - When you were the leader, did you think your partner chose willingness?
    - What was easy or hard about practicing "willing hands"?
    - Why would you practice "willing hands" in your day?

Modifications for higher developmental level

1. Explain that "sometimes things happen in our life that we don't really like; and, if we are **wilful**, we whine and complain and do things that may make the problem worse."

2. Explain: "A more helpful way to manage things we don't like is to choose **willingness**, we accept what happens and do what we need to do to get through the situation."

3. Continue: "An example of **wilfulness** might be that our teacher tells us to line up for art class. You want to finish building your Lego creation, and so you stay in your chair and refuse to leave. You complain about having to leave and argue with your teacher. Now you and your class are late to art."

4. Additional examples of **wilfulness** include:
    - Not being willing to listen to a friend give an explanation
    - Doing a house chore for your parents while complaining and feeling angry the entire time

- Sitting down and not moving from the spot when you are mad.

5. An example of **willingness** would be to accept that it is time to move on, even though you don't want to, and find time later in the day to come back to your Lego creation. Now you and your class get to participate in art the entire time. Give the additional explanation of **willingness** as responding to what happens in life appropriately and effectively. Explain that you do not have to like it, and you can still do what is needed.

6. Offer an opportunity for students to practice body postures that might demonstrate willfulness and then willingness.

7. Engage in the mirror dance. Encourage students to use both willful and willing body postures.

8. Prompt students to partner up or assign partners for each student.

9. Explain: "We can practice willingness by following the lead of a partner in a dance."

10. Invite students to pick a leader or assign a leader for the dance.

11. Invite students to make different movements by lifting arms up and down, in and out, around in circles, or any movements they choose.

12. Invite students to practice willingness by following their partner without complaining and responding to the movements as best as they can.

13. Play the song for students to practice willingness for 1 minute 25 seconds, then pause the music.

14. Explain: "An easy way to help ourselves feel more willing is to hold our hands out in front of us in an open position with our palms facing up. This is called **willing hands**."

15. Explain: "In this song we are going to practice willing hands every time we hear the words 'Try everything' in the chorus." (Or use any repeated lyric.)

16. Start the song, then pause at 1 minute 25 seconds (when the lyrics say "try everything") and invite students to practice "willing hands."

17. Play through the song a second time after prompting the students to switch the leader and follower. Remind them to listen to the cue for "willing hands."

18. Discussion questions:
    - Did you demonstrate willingness while following your partner?
    - When you were the leader, did you think your partner chose willingness?
    - What was easy or hard about practicing "willing hands"?
    - Why would you practice "willing hands" in your day?

✿ FLOAT ON BY

Module: Distress Tolerance

Skill addressed
Mindfulness of Current Thought

Summary
The main goal of this exercise and song is to teach the concept of detaching from thoughts and letting them pass by, instead of getting stuck on negative thoughts when we are feeling upsetting emotions.

Materials needed

- Song lyrics and/or video to "This is just a thought" (in the lesson overview) and means to play the song/video (recording available at https://www.youtube.com/playlist?list=PL0jguhoPs0m6qrlhhTR7P4PPtz7wuicy1 or by scanning the QR code in the Appendix)
- Picture of clouds
- Picture of a thought bubble cloud
- Scarves or ribbon (white, gray, blue, light blue)

Lesson overview

1. Ask the children: "Have you ever felt like no matter what you do or how hard you try, you just can't get a thought out of your head?"
2. Present the picture of the cloud.
3. Explain that "in the same way clouds pass by in the sky, we can learn to let our thoughts pass by in our head, instead of letting them get stuck."
4. Present the picture of the thought bubble cloud.
5. Explain: "We can imagine that we watch the thoughts pass through our head, just like we watch the clouds pass by in the sky."
6. Play the video of the song "This is just a thought" for the students to hear or read it like a poem while playing soft music.
7. Pass out scarves or ribbons and ask the students to move them like clouds or thoughts floating across the sky.
8. Play the video again and model movements with the students.
9. Review the song, singing with the students.
10. Invite the students to listen again to the video and sing along with the chorus.

This is just a thought

C   F
I have a thought it can float on by.
C   G
Just like the clouds way up in the sky.
C   F
I watch the thought come and I watch it go.
C   G   C
Where does it come from, where will it go?

Chorus
This is just a thought, just a thought, just a thought. This is just a thought,
just a thought.
This is just a thought, just a thought, just a thought. This is just a thought,
just a thought.

C   F
My thoughts are not all of who I can be.
C   G
I only watch them to see what I see.
C   F
I do not have to act out every thought.
C   G   C
I can just notice as they float by.

Chorus
This is just a thought, just a thought, just a thought. This is just a thought,
just a thought.
This is just a thought, just a thought, just a thought. This is just a thought,
just a thought.

11. Discussion questions:
    - Have you ever watched clouds pass in the sky?
    - Can you imagine your thoughts like the clouds?
    - Can you remember how to sing the chorus? Show me.
    - Do you always have to act out the thought that comes into your mind?
    - Do you notice a thought you are having right now?

EMOTION REGULATION

Emotions give us information about the world by communicating to ourselves what is going on in any given situation, motivating us to act quickly, and they can also communicate to others. Emotions therefore are very important for us to have as humans! Sometimes we can feel emotions in ways that feel too "big" or too painful, or do not quite line up with the facts of a situation, prompting us to act in ways that are not in our "wise mind," i.e. effective or in line with our goals and values. Learning about what makes up an emotion, being able to put emotions into words, recognizing what may influence or prompt emotions, changing unhelpful emotions, and increasing positive emotions are all key components of emotion regulation. Emotion regulation does not mean getting rid of emotion, suppressing emotions, or the polar opposite of allowing our emotions to rule freely; by naming and understanding our emotions we gain the control to decide how to proceed in any given moment via skills to help us either increase or decrease the intensity of an emotion. Emotion regulation skills can also include preventative skills aimed at reducing our vulnerabilities to being in "emotion mind," therefore helping to prevent "big" emotions before they even start.

Concepts and skills in this section include:

- Identifying emotions: The purpose of emotion
- Changing emotions: Opposite action, problem solving, and check the facts
- Decreasing vulnerabilities: Accumulating the positives, build mastery, cope ahead, reducing emotion mind through PLEASE
- Managing really hard emotions: Mindfulness of current emotion.

WHAT DO MY EMOTIONS DO?

Module: Emotion Regulation

Skill addressed

Purpose of Emotions

Summary

The main goal of this activity is to identify the three purposes of emotions: a sign to give us information, a way to communicate with others, and to prepare us to take action.

Materials needed

- Lyrics (included in the lesson overview) for the song about purposes of emotions
- Optional craft activity materials: Paper plates, markers, photos or printed pictures of a variety of emoji faces or children making different faces to represent emotions, popsicle sticks, glue

Lesson preparation

- Write the following three purposes of emotions on a whiteboard:
  - A sign to give us information
  - A tool to communicate
  - To prepare us to take action

Lesson overview

1. Explain: "All emotions are important. Emotions that we like having are important and those that are uncomfortable and we don't like having are just as important too."
2. Explain to students that "today we will learn a song that tells us what emotions do for us."
3. These song lyrics are to be sung to the tune of "Oats, Peas, Beans and Barley Grow," a traditional British-Canadian-American folk song. Sing the first stanza[1] and then explain that "emotions show us something is

1 A stanza is a group of lines.

happening—a sign." Sing the second stanza: "emotions communicate to us and help us talk to others." Sing the last stanza: "emotions also get us ready to act."

What do my emotions do?
What do my emotions do?
I name and notice what I feel.
What do my emotions do?

My emotion is a sign.
My emotion is a sign.
It tells me something's happening.
My emotion is a sign.

My face and body changes.
My face and body changes.
Share with others how I feel.
My face and body changes.

Emotions get me ready to act.
Emotions get me ready to act.
I respond to what's around.
Emotions get me ready to act.

4. After singing, review with students that emotions give us information, communicate with others, and get us ready to act.
5. An optional activity is to invite students to create a sign for different emotions. Pass out paper plates and pictures of emojis or different representations of emotions. Have students name the emotion indicated and glue it to the paper plate. An optional discussion is to talk about the face and body changes they noticed that communicated the pictured emotion.
6. Assist students in gluing the paper plate to the popsicle stick. Invite students to hold the sign up. Sing through the song and prompt them to hold up the sign when they hear the lyrics "sign" in the song.
7. Invite students to sing along with the song again with you.
8. Discussion questions:
   - Do you ever think of your emotions as a sign—like a stop sign or a walk sign that says it is okay to go?

- Have you ever seen the way someone looks and been able to guess what they are feeling?
- Have you ever noticed a feeling and then noticed what happened that caused you to feel that way?
- Can you name any of the three things emotions do for us?

Modifications for higher developmental level

1. Explain: "All emotions are important. Emotions that we like having are important and those that are uncomfortable and we don't like having are just as important too."
2. Explain to students that "today we will learn a song that tells us what emotions do for us."
3. These song lyrics are to be sung to the tune of "Oats, Peas, Beans and Barley Grow," a traditional British-Canadian-American folk song. Sing the first stanza and then explain that "emotions show us something is happening—a sign." Sing the second stanza: "emotions communicate to us and help us talk to others." Sing the last stanza: "emotions also get us ready to act."

What do my emotions do?
What do my emotions do?
I name and notice what I feel.
What do my emotions do?

My emotion is a sign.
My emotion is a sign.
It tells me something's happening.
My emotion is a sign.

My face and body changes.
My face and body changes.
Share with others how I feel.
My face and body changes.

Emotions get me ready to act.
Emotions get me ready to act.
I respond to what's around.
Emotions get me ready to act.

4. After singing, review with students that emotions give us information, communicate with others, and get us ready to act.

5. During the crafting part of the session, you could have students draw a picture of different emotion faces and then try to name the emotion drawn by a peer.

6. Discussion questions:

   - What face or body changes indicate when a person is feeling sad? Mad? Excited? Happy?

   - Tell me about a time you noticed your body get ready to act when you were feeling an emotion. (Possible examples: feeling scared or surprised to move away from danger, or feeling happy and celebrating with others.)

   - Can you name the three ways emotions affect us?

✿ NAME MY EMOTIONS

Module: Emotion Regulation

Skill addressed
Understanding Emotions

Summary
The main goal of this activity is to identify the different emotions one may experience.

Materials needed

- The means to play a recorded song—"The Scribble SPOT Feeling Song" by Diane Alber is recommended. It is based on Alber's book *A Little SPOT of Feelings: Emotion Detective* and links emotions to colors
- Six sheets of paper and markers of different colors (yellow, red, pink, green, gray, orange)
- Lyrics for the songs you are using

Lesson overview

1. Explain that "there are many emotions that we can feel every day."
2. Talk with students about the importance of noticing and identifying emotions when you are having them so you can better understand what you are experiencing.
3. Tell students you will listen to a song and try to identify all of the emotions you hear in the song. Tell them the song will describe colors and match them with emotions. State: "We will write the emotions on individual pieces of paper, using the colors corresponding to the song."
4. Play the song "The Scribble SPOT Feeling Song." Either pause the song after each emotion and write down the emotion or play through the song and then review the emotions.
5. After the song, identify each emotion with the students. Ask if they can think of any other emotions not listed that they have experienced.
6. Choose five emotion names. On the pieces of paper for each emotion write down a corresponding body change for each emotion (e.g. sad—cry; happy—smile; angry—scream; afraid—hide; worried—bite your nails).

7. Sing the following song to the tune of "Itsy Bitsy Spider," using one emotion each time with the corresponding body change the students identified.

Name my emotions, notice how I feel.
One way I might feel is the emotion _____(sad)_____.
When I'm feeling __(sad)_____ I want to __(cry)_____.
Name my emotions, notice how I feel.

8. Discussion questions:
   - Have you ever experienced each of these emotions we sang about?
   - Do you notice when you have a change in your emotions?
   - What emotions are easy for you to name?
   - What emotions are more difficult for you to name?

Modifications for higher developmental level
MATERIALS NEEDED

- A song that uses feeling words like "Joy" by Andy Grammer and the means to play the song

LESSON OVERVIEW

1. Introduce the importance of observing and describing emotions to identify them.
2. Play the song "Joy" by Andy Grammer or another song that uses feeling words, and have students write down all of the emotion names they hear in the song.
3. Ask students if they can think of other emotion names to add to the list.
4. Play a background rhythmic beat for the students using a recorded karaoke beat.
5. Invite students to fill in words in the following rap:

When I'm sad,
I want to __(be alone)_____.
I feel it in my __(body part, e.g. heart)___.

When I'm glad,
When I'm glad,

I want to___(laugh)____.
I feel it in my __(body part, e.g. face)___.

When I'm mad,
I want to___(yell)_____.
I feel it in my __(body part, e.g. shoulders)__.

When I'm worried,
I want to ___(hide)_____.
I feel it in my __(body part, e.g. stomach)__.

6. Discussion questions:
   - Have you ever experienced the emotions we rapped about?
   - Do you notice in your body when you have a change in your emotions?
   - What emotions are easy for you to name?
   - What emotions are more difficult for you to name?
   - Which part of the rap was easy to write?
   - Which part of the rap was hard to write?

✿ MUSICAL CHAIRS MEET MY FEELINGS

Module: Emotion Regulation

Skill addressed
Understanding Emotions

Summary
The main goal of this activity is to understand how our body moves and responds to emotions.

Materials needed

+ A song of your choice (examples include: "Better When I'm Dancing" by Meghan Trainor; "Permission to Dance" by BTS; "Sunday Best" by Surfaces) and the means to play it. Choose music easy to dance to with a strong beat
+ A chair for each student
+ Pieces of red paper, blue paper, and yellow paper

Lesson preparation

+ Cue audio
+ Place chairs in a circle facing out
+ Place one colored piece of paper on each chair, alternating red, blue, and yellow
+ Keep one of each colored paper for the teacher

Lesson overview

1. Explain that when we have different emotions we might experience the emotion in our bodies. This is what we call "how we feel."
2. When we notice how our body is feeling and how we are acting or want to act, it can help us identify the emotion we are experiencing.
3. Today we are going to practice making different movements with our bodies for different emotions.
4. Explain that the different colored paper represents different emotions. Red represents anger; blue represents sadness; yellow represents happiness.
5. Invite the students to each stand by a chair and walk around the chairs

when the music is playing. Instruct them to stop and sit on a chair closest to them when they hear the music stop.

6. Explain that when the music stops, the teacher will hold up one piece of paper. The students with the matching paper will then act out the emotion it represents. For example, the teacher holds up red. Every student sitting on red will do a movement to represent feeling angry. The next time the teacher holds up blue. Every student sitting on a blue paper will do a movement to represent feeling sad.

7. Continue until students have had the opportunity to express each of the emotions.

8. Discussion questions:
   - Did you make a different movement for each emotion?
   - What was easy about making the movements?
   - What was hard about making each movement?
   - Can you tell me about a time you felt angry (sad, or happy)? Can you tell me how your body felt? Can you tell me what you did with your body?

Modifications for higher developmental level
MATERIALS NEEDED

◆ A chair for each student
◆ Pieces of red paper, blue paper, yellow paper, orange paper, green paper, pink paper, and purple paper
◆ Means to play a song of your choice (examples include: "Better When I'm Dancing" by Meghan Trainor; "Permission to Dance" by BTS; "Sunday Best" by Surfaces)

LESSON PREPARATION

◆ Place chairs in a circle facing out
◆ Place one colored piece of paper on each chair, alternating between the five colors
◆ Keep one of each colored paper for the teacher
◆ Cue song of your choice

LESSON OVERVIEW

1. Explain that when we have different emotions we might experience the emotion in our bodies. This is what we call "how we feel."

2. When we notice how our body is feeling and how we are acting or want to act, it can help us identify the emotion we are experiencing.

3. Today we are going to practice making different movements with our bodies for different emotions.

4. Explain that the different colored paper represents different emotions. Red represents anger; blue represents sadness; yellow represents happiness; orange represents anxiety; green represents disgust; pink represents love; purple represents embarrassment. Elicit other color and emotion pairs from the students such as envy, jealousy, and excitement.

5. Invite the students to each stand by a chair and walk around the chairs when the music is playing. Instruct them to stop and sit on a chair closest to them when they hear the music stop.

6. Explain that when the music stops, the teacher will hold up one piece of paper. The students with the matching paper will then act out the emotion it represents. For example, the teacher holds up red. Every student sitting on red will do a movement to represent feeling angry. The next time the teacher holds up blue. Every student sitting on a blue paper will do a movement to represent feeling sad.

7. Continue until students have had the opportunity to express each of the emotions.

8. Discussion questions:
    ▪ Do you always do the same action when you feel an emotion?
    ▪ Have you ever noticed yourself doing an action before you knew what emotion you felt?
    ▪ How can noticing your body help identify what emotion you are feeling?

❀ MY BODY, MY EMOTIONS

Module: Emotion Regulation

Skill addressed
Understanding Emotions

Summary
The main goal of this activity is to identify emotions and where we experience them in our body.

Materials needed

◆ Outline of Gingerbread Body (small: 3–4 to a page, or large: 1 to a page—see the end of the activity for an outline, you can also download a copy to print from www.jkp.com/catalogue/book/9781805013211)
◆ Markers, crayons, colored pencils
◆ Playlist of instrumental music (1 or 2 selections for each emotion—happiness/joy, sadness, anger, scared/anxious, etc.) and the means to play it. Examples (you can also search instrumental + emotion in your favorite music streaming service):
  ▪ Happy/Excited
    – "Walking on Sunshine" (acoustic or instrumental)—Katrina and the Waves
    – "Here Comes the Sun" (instrumental)—The Beatles
    – "Flight of the Bumblebee"—Rimsky-Korsakov (high energy and fun)
  ▪ Sad/Reflective
    – "Moonlight Sonata" (First Movement)—Beethoven
    – "Adagio for Strings"—Samuel Barber (emotional depth)
    – "The Swan"—Saint-Saëns (gentle and poignant)
    – Soft piano improvisations, such as those by Yiruma ("River Flows in You")
  ▪ Angry/Frustrated
    – "Mars, The Bringer of War"—Gustav Holst (intense energy)
    – "In the Hall of the Mountain King"—Edvard Grieg (escalating intensity)
  ▪ Scared/Anxious
    – "Danse Macabre"—Saint-Saëns (creepy but playful)
    – "Toccata and Fugue in D Minor"—J.S. Bach (spooky tension)

Lesson preparation

◆ Bring up or make a list of instrumental songs for each emotion. Search your preferred music service, such as YouTube or Spotify (i.e. sad instrumental songs)

◆ Have copies of the Gingerbread Body for each student (start with the four main emotions—happy, sad, angry, scared)

Lesson overview

1. Introduce the concept of emotions being experienced in our body which we call feelings. "Sometimes, when we feel a big emotion, we see it on our face. Like when I'm happy, I might smile—everyone show me your biggest Happy Smile!" Go through each emotion and have students show their emotion faces (sad face, angry face, scared face). "Our big emotions might want to be shown through other parts of our body. If we are scared, we might shake; or if we are angry, we might stomp our feet."

2. Introduce the music: "We are going to listen to a piece of music. While you listen, think about what emotion this music sounds like to you."

3. Play instrumental "Happy" music selection.

4. Continue for the other three emotions—sad, angry, and scared.

5. Discussion questions following each of the songs:
   ▪ What emotion did the music make you think of?
   ▪ What color do you think this emotion might be?
   ▪ Where do you feel this emotion in your body?
   ▪ Can you show me what that looks like? (e.g. clenched fists for anger, or tears for sad)

6. "Now, we are going to listen again. While the music is playing, I want you to color the part of the body that you feel this emotion on the Gingerbread body."

Modifications for higher developmental level
MATERIALS NEEDED

◆ Playlist of instrumental music to expand on the list of emotions above, one or two selections for each emotion:
   ▪ Curious/Playful
      – "The Entertainer"—Scott Joplin

- – "Peter and the Wolf" Themes—Prokofiev (playful storytelling tones)
  - – "Carnival of the Animals" (fossil or kangaroo movements)—Saint-Saëns
- ■ Brave/Confident
  - – "Eye of the Tiger" (instrumental)—Survivor
  - – "Ode to Joy"—Beethoven
  - – "We Are the Champions" (instrumental)—Queen
  - – Triumphant orchestral themes—Think "Superman" or "Star Wars" instrumentals
- ■ Calm/Peaceful
  - – "Clair de Lune"—Claude Debussy
  - – "Weightless"—Marconi Union
  - – "Somewhere Over the Rainbow" (instrumental)—Soothing ukulele or piano versions
  - – "Aquarium"—Saint-Saëns (magical and serene)

LESSON OVERVIEW

1. Introduce the concept of emotions being experienced in our body which we call feelings. "Sometimes, when we feel a big emotion, we see it on our face. Like when I'm happy, I might smile—everyone show me your biggest Happy Smile!" Go through each emotion and have students show their emotion faces (sad face, angry face, scared face). "Our big emotions might want to be shown through other parts of our body. If we are scared, we might shake; or if we are angry, we might stomp our feet."
2. Introduce the music: "We are going to listen to a piece of music. While you listen, think about what emotion this music sounds like to you."
3. Play instrumental "Happy" music selection.
4. Continue for the other three emotions—sad, angry, and scared.
5. Discussion questions following each of the songs:
   - ■ What emotion did the music make you think of?
   - ■ What color do you think this emotion might be?
   - ■ Where do you feel this emotion in your body?
   - ■ Can you show me what that looks like? (e.g. clenched fists for anger, or tears for sad)
6. Explore other emotions/feelings such as curious, calm/peaceful, brave/confident, disappointed, frustrated, jealous, embarrassed, envy, disgust, excited, etc.

7. "Now, we are going to listen again. While the music is playing, I want you to color the part of the body where you feel this emotion on the Gingerbread body." Discuss how we can feel more than one emotion at a time, and sometimes the emotions can become tangled. When we can name our emotions, we can untangle them.

8. Have students come up with a particular movement that demonstrates each emotion—they can dance with that movement or body part when each example of music is played.

✿ CHECKING THE FACTS

Module: Emotion Regulation

Skill addressed
Changing Emotions: Check the Facts

Summary
The main goal of this activity is to practice checking the facts in order to accurately describe a situation before making decisions rather than simply reacting from emotional urges.

Materials needed

+ Whiteboard, dry-erase markers or smartboard
+ Pictures of children displaying various emotions
+ Objects (animals, colors, shapes, etc.)

Lesson preparation

+ Have your pictures/objects ready to show after singing the song

Lesson overview

1. Teach the song to students to the tune of the "Addams Family Theme" by Vic Mizzy & His Orchestra. Clapping can be substituted for snapping.

    Checking the Facts (snap, snap)
    Checking the Facts (snap, snap)
    Checking the Facts, Checking the Facts, Checking the Facts (snap, snap)

2. Define the word fact: A fact is something that is true about a situation. For example (hold out an object, e.g. a green frog): "If I said this is a black cat, is that true? No…what is it actually?" (a green frog!)
3. Play a game singing the song, then presenting an object. Make a statement that is either true or not true about the object. Have the students give a thumbs up if the statement is true, or a thumbs down if the statement is not true.
4. After a few rounds with concrete objects, try a few rounds with scenarios

of situations where an emotion that a child is having may, or may not, fit the facts. For example, a child can be angry at a classmate thinking that they "stole" their pencil when the classmate may have thought the pencil was theirs; a child feeling afraid to present in front of the class thinking they will be made fun of even though they've prepared thoroughly and they've never been made fun of by these classmates before; or a child feeling sad that their parent told them they have to wait until after dinner to eat the cookies they just baked. Can the students "Check the facts" of these emotions?

5. Discussion questions:
    ▪ When does sadness fit the facts? When does fear fit the facts? Anger?
    ▪ Why is it important to check the facts of a situation?
    ▪ Could our emotions change if the facts are not true?

Modifications for higher developmental level

1. 1. Lesson preparation: Draw a triangle on the board and label one side "Sensations"; the second side "Thoughts"; and the third side "Actions."
2. Teach the song to students to the tune of the "Addams Family Theme." Clapping can be substituted for snapping.

Chorus:
Checking the Facts
Checking the Facts
Checking the Facts, Checking the Facts, Checking the Facts

Verse:
Name the emotion
The waves feel like the ocean
What started the situation
And how did I react?

Chorus:
Checking the Facts
Checking the Facts
Checking the Facts, Checking the Facts, Checking the Facts

3. Explain that emotions, thoughts, and actions are different. Sometimes we have emotions that come over us like a wave.

4. Those emotions are part of a triangle.

5. Draw a triangle and label the triangle as you explain: "On the first side we have sensations. These are the physical urges and feelings we experience within an emotion. On the second side, we have thoughts. Sometimes our thoughts are facts and sometimes they are interpretations, assumptions, or judgments. On the third side, we have actions—our reactions and responses. Sometimes we must check the facts to manage our reactions."

6. Ask the students to share a recent time when they felt sad or angry.

7. Go through a simple Emotion Diary with students. Make three columns and label them:
    ▪ Facts of the event
    ▪ How I reacted (What emotions did I feel, what thoughts did I have?)
    ▪ Was the reaction helpful?

8. Walk through as many situations or emotions as time allows.

9. Discussion questions:
    ▪ What happens if I react to an interpretation as a fact?
    ▪ Why is it important to check the facts of a situation?
    ▪ Could our emotions change if the facts are false? For example, you are angry at your friend thinking that they took your cookies at lunch but the fact is that your mom forgot to pack your cookies.

ACT OPPOSITE

Module: Emotion Regulation

Skill addressed

Changing Emotions: Opposite Action

Summary

The main goal of this activity is to identify an action urge and an opposite action for an emotion.

Materials needed

- Hula hoops or tape to make circles on the floor
- Labels written on paper:
  - Emotion
  - Action
  - Action Urge
  - Opposite Action
- Song lyrics (included in the lesson overview)

Lesson overview

1. Put out two large hula hoops and mark one Emotion and the other Action.
2. Explain that "when we have an emotion we often act in a certain way after the emotion."
3. Share: "When feeling angry we might want to hit, punch, throw something, or yell. When feeling sad we might want to hide away, pout by ourself, or push people away. When feeling scared we might want to run or avoid."
4. Sing the following lyrics to the tune of "Open Shut Them," a nursery rhyme that can be found online.

   Emotion and action
   emotion and action.
   I feel then I want to act.
   Opposite action; opposite action
   When it doesn't fit the facts.

5. Ask what an opposite is and explain if needed. Explain: "When emotions don't fit the facts it helps change your emotion to act in the opposite way of how you feel." For example, if you feel scared of a mouse across the yard from you because you think it will bite you, your emotion does not fit the facts. The fact is the mouse cannot bite you from across the yard.
6. Sing the lyrics again and add the additional lyrics about possible opposite actions.

    Fast or slow; fast or slow. Are opposite ways to act.
    Loud or quiet; loud or quiet. Are opposite ways to act.
    Hide or be brave; hide or be brave. Are opposite ways to act.
    Push away or get close; push away or get close. Are opposite ways to act.

7. Add two additional circles to the floor moving off of the paper that says action. Label one "action urge" and one "opposite action."
8. Have children stand on or near the circle that is labeled "emotion" and name an emotion (e.g. sad).
9. Sing the lyrics: "Emotion and action; emotion and action. I feel then I want to act."
10. Prompt the children to move to the circle that is labeled "action." Prompt discussion of possible action urges for sad including getting quiet, hiding, pushing people away. Have students point or move to the circle labeled "action urge."
11. Sing the lyrics: "Opposite action; opposite action when it doesn't fit the facts."
12. Use words for the action urge named previously by the children for the emotions given and sing as an opposite within the lyrics of the song. (E.g. "Quiet or talk, quiet or talk. Are opposite ways to act." "Hide or be brave, hide or be brave. Are opposite ways to act." "Push away or get close. Are opposite ways to act.")
13. Repeat for as many emotions as desired.
14. Discussion questions:
    - Can you think of an action you might want to do after feeling sad? Angry? Scared?
    - Have you ever felt an emotion then done one of those actions? What happened?
    - When you feel that emotion again is there an "opposite action" you could do instead?
    - What is easy about using opposite action?

- What is hard about using opposite action?

Modifications for higher developmental level
LESSON OVERVIEW

1. Put out two large hula hoops and mark one Emotion and the other Action.
2. Explain that "when we have an emotion we often act in a certain way after the emotion."
3. Share: "When feeling angry we might want to hit, punch, throw something, or yell. When feeling sad we might want to hide away, pout by ourself, or push people away. When feeling scared we might want to run or avoid."
4. Sing the following lyrics to the tune of "Open Shut Them."

   Emotion and action
   emotion and action.
   I feel then I want to act.
   Opposite action; opposite action
   When it doesn't fit the facts.

5. Ask what an opposite is and explain if needed. Explain: "When emotions don't fit the facts it helps change your emotion to act in the opposite way of how you feel." For example, if you feel scared of a mouse across the yard from you because you think it will bite you, your emotion does not fit the facts. The fact is the mouse cannot bite you from across the yard.
6. Sing the lyrics again and add the additional lyrics about possible opposite actions.

   Fast or slow; fast or slow. Are opposite ways to act.
   Loud or quiet; loud or quiet. Are opposite ways to act.
   Hide or be brave; hide or be brave. Are opposite ways to act.
   Push away or get close; push away or get close. Are opposite ways to act.

7. Add two additional circles to the floor moving off of the paper that says action. Label one "action urge" and one "opposite action."
8. Have children stand on or near the circle that is labeled "emotion" and name an emotion (e.g. sad).
9. Sing the lyrics: "Emotion and action; emotion and action. I feel then I want to act."

10. Prompt the children to move to the circle that is labeled "action." Prompt discussion of possible action urges for sad including getting quiet, hiding, pushing people away. Have students point or move to the circle labeled "action urge."

11. Sing the lyrics: "Opposite action; opposite action when it doesn't fit the facts."

12. Use words for the action urge named previously by the children for the emotions given and sing as an opposite within the lyrics of the song. (E.g. "Quiet or talk, quiet or talk. Are opposite ways to act." "Hide or be brave, hide or be brave. Are opposite ways to act." "Push away or get close. Are opposite ways to act.") Additional examples of opposite action: taking a walk, talking with a parent or trusted adult, writing a letter, calling a friend when sad, or facing something that scares you when you know it is safe.

13. Repeat for as many emotions as desired.

14. Discussion questions:

   - Can you think of an action you might want to do after feeling sad? Angry? Scared? Nervous? Worried? Jealous? Ashamed?
   - Have you ever felt an emotion then done one of those actions? What happened?
   - When you feel that emotion again is there an "opposite action" you could do instead?
   - What is easy about using opposite action?
   - What is hard about using opposite action?

✿ I'VE BEEN WORKING ON A PROBLEM

Module: Emotion Regulation

Skill addressed
Changing Emotions: Problem Solving

Summary
The main goal of this activity is to identify a problem and find creative solutions that solve the identified problem, thus changing the original, undesired emotion.

Materials needed

◆ Smartboard or whiteboard and markers
◆ Choice wheel (blank or filled out)
  ▪ A choice wheel is a decision-making spinner. It's a tool that can help with decision-making by breaking down options into visual segments. It's like a game show type spinner where you can put different choices into the different segments. You may find templates or apps online to make your own
◆ Music sticks or shakers for half the class

Lesson overview

1. Teach the song by singing to the tune of the traditional song "I've Been Working on the Railroad." Can pat a steady beat on knees while singing:

   I've been working on a problem all the live long day
   I've been working on a problem and I don't know what to say
   Can you help me solve a problem?
   I don't know what to do
   I need to find the solution
   Which one should I choose?

   What can I do? (hands open, palms up)
   What do I do? (hands open, palms up)
   How can I solve this problem? (Point to brain)
   What can I do? (hands open, palms up)

What can I do? (hands open, palms up)
Which one should I choose? (Point to brain)

2. Pass out instruments to use while singing the song.
3. Only pass out enough for half the class.
4. Pause long enough for students to recognize that there are not enough for everyone. Guide them through problem solving: "Uh-oh…we have a problem! What's our problem? (We don't have enough instruments for everyone.) What can we do? What are some possible solutions to fix our problem?"
5. Write solutions on the choice wheel.
6. Sing through the second half of the song ("What can I do…").
7. Guide the class into choosing a solution and trying it. Then sing the song with the solution in place (taking turns/sharing, etc.).
8. Discussion questions:
   - Did the solution/choice work?
   - How did it feel to make this choice?
   - Could another choice have worked? If so, which one?

Modifications for higher developmental level

1. Teach the song by singing to the tune of the traditional song "I've Been Working on the Railroad." Can pat a steady beat on knees while singing:

I've been working on a problem all the live long day
I've been working on a problem and I don't know what to say
Can you help me solve a problem?
I don't know what to do
I need to find the solution
Which one should I choose?

What can I do? (hands open, palms up)
What do I do? (hands open, palms up)
How can I solve this problem? (Point to brain)
What can I do? (hands open, palms up)
What can I do? (hands open, palms up)
Which one should I choose? (Point to brain)

2. Pass out instruments to use while singing the song.

3. Only pass out enough for half the class.
4. Pause long enough for students to recognize that there are not enough for everyone. Guide them through problem solving: "Uh-oh…we have a problem! What's our problem? (We don't have enough instruments for everyone.) What can we do? What are some possible solutions to fix our problem?"
5. Write solutions on the choice wheel.
6. Sing through the second half of the song ("What can I do…").
7. Guide the class into choosing a solution and trying it. Then sing the song with the solution in place (taking turns/sharing, etc.).
8. Now get a hula hoop. Have students stand in a line holding hands (shoulder to shoulder). Problem: how do we move the hula hoop from the beginning of the line to the end without letting go of hands?
9. Discussion questions:
   - Did the solution/choice work?
   - How did it feel to make this choice?
   - Could another choice have worked? If so, which one?

✿ FIND THE FUN!

Module: Emotion Regulation

Skill addressed
Decreasing Vulnerabilities: Accumulating Positives in the Short Term

Summary
The main goal of this activity is to identify five enjoyable activities to add to a "fun list" that students can use to accumulate positives.

Materials needed

- Song lyrics (included in the lesson overview)
- Paper or whiteboard to record ideas for "Fun List"
- Optional: instrumental version of "London Bridge Is Falling Down" and means to play it

Lesson overview

1. Explain that "when we participate in activities that bring us happiness and joy, we can help keep our life balanced. If we have more opportunities to feel happiness, we will be stronger on days when an unwanted emotion pops up."
2. Explain that "activities that build joy and happiness in our lives are things we like to do. After we do these activities we feel like we want to smile and laugh and keep doing the activities."
3. Invite children to think of some examples of activities they enjoy to create what we will call a "Fun List." Create a list together. In group settings, remind children they might like some activities that their friends don't like just as their friends might like something that they do not like. Share with them that it is okay to have different "Fun Lists."
4. Once a list is created, invite children to listen to this song to identify when to find the "Fun List." Sing the song for the children to the tune of the traditional children's song "London Bridge Is Falling Down." Invite children to sing along with the chorus once they learn it.

Let us have some fun today
Hip hip hip; hip hooray!

Jump and dance and sing and play
Build joy today.

When you are feeling sad,
And you want to feel glad.
Go find the fun list.
Enjoy the day!

Let us have some fun today
Hip hip hip; hip hooray!
Jump and dance and sing and play
Build joy today.

When you are feeling mad,
And you want to feel glad.
Go find the fun list.
Enjoy the day!

Let us have some fun today
Hip hip hip; hip hooray!
Jump and dance and sing and play
Build joy today.

When you are feeling scared,
And you want to feel better.
Go find the fun list.
Enjoy the day!

Let us have some fun today
Hip hip hip; hip hooray!
Jump and dance and sing and play
Build joy today.

5. Offer a copy of the "Fun List" for children to take home.
6. Discussion questions:
   - Will you tell me about a time where you were feeling sad and you did something fun to help yourself feel happier?
   - Do you think you could use one of these activities one time every day?

- If you tried to choose one of these things to do every day, how would your feelings change?
- Can you add other activities to your "Fun List"?
- Who can you tell about your "Fun List"?

Modifications for higher developmental level

1. Explain that "when we participate in activities that bring us happiness and joy, we can help keep our life balanced. If we have more opportunities to feel happiness, we will be stronger on days when an unwanted emotion pops up."
2. Explain that "activities that build joy and happiness in our lives are things we like to do. After we do these activities we feel like we want to smile and laugh and keep doing the activities."
3. Talk about accumulating positives like a scale and increasing the positive experiences in your life so when a negative emotion comes it will not tip the scale farther to one side. Have the students create a list of fun activities as a group.
4. Sing through the lyrics in a chant style with an optional background beat from an electronic keyboard or a background beat found online.

Let us have some fun today
Hip hip hip; hip hooray!
Jump and dance and sing and play
Build joy today.

When you are feeling sad,
And you want to feel glad.
Go find the fun list.
Enjoy the day!

Let us have some fun today
Hip hip hip; hip hooray!
Jump and dance and sing and play
Build joy today.

When you are feeling mad,
And you want to feel glad.

Go find the fun list.
Enjoy the day!

Let us have some fun today
Hip hip hip; hip hooray!
Jump and dance and sing and play
Build joy today.

When you are feeling scared,
And you want to feel better.
Go find the fun list.
Enjoy the day!

Let us have some fun today
Hip hip hip; hip hooray!
Jump and dance and sing and play
Build joy today.

5. Discussion questions:
   - Tell me about a time where you were feeling sad and you did something fun to help yourself feel happier.
   - Do you think you could use one of these activities one time every day?
   - If you tried to choose one of these things to do every day, how would your feelings change?
   - Can you add other activities to your "Fun List"?
   - Who can you tell about your "Fun List"?
   - Have you ever had an experience where you tried to balance the scale of negative and positive emotions? How did you use a "Fun List"?
   - What could you do if it happened again?

✽ MAKE NEW FRIENDS

Module: Emotion Regulation

Skill addressed
Decreasing Vulnerabilities: Accumulating Positives in the Long Term

Summary
The main goal of this activity is to make changes in our lives so that positives can happen more often through learning to set goals that are in line with our values.

Materials needed

◆ Recording of "Make New Friends," an American folk song (public domain, so easy to look up), and the means to play the song
◆ The following lyrics:
   Make new friends
   But keep the old
   One is silver,
   And the other gold.

Lesson overview

1. Ask: "How does it feel to have friends? Do our friends make us feel good for just a minute, or for a long time? Do you think you value, or really care about, having friends?"
2. Say: "Making friends isn't always easy, and the reward can be a lot of fun. If I really care about friendships, what are some things I can do to reach the goal of making a friend?"
3. Make a list of student suggestions.
4. Ask: "What is the first step?"
5. "We are going to learn a song to remind us of the importance of taking the first steps to make new friends and to keep friends we have had for a long time."
6. Teach song "Make New Friends" from the recording.

Modifications for higher developmental level

1. Ask: "How does it feel to have friends? Do our friends make us feel good for just a minute, or for a long time? Do you think you value, or really care about, having friends?"

2. Say: "Making friends isn't always easy, and the reward can be a lot of fun. If I really care about friendships, what are some things I can do to reach the goal of making a friend?"

3. Make a list of student suggestions.

4. Ask: "What is the first step?"

5. "We are going to learn a song to remind us of the importance of taking the first steps to make new friends and to keep friends we have had for a long time."

6. Teach song "Make New Friends" from the recording.

7. Ask: "If our goal is to keep new friends, what are things we can do to keep working on that friendship?"

8. Make a list of student suggestions.

9. Ask: "What is the first step?"

10. "We are going to work on our new song and add a challenge to sing it as a round. Our first step was to learn the song."

11. Ask students: "If our new goal is to sing it in a round, what is the next step?" Get ideas.

12. If the students didn't get into two groups, say: "Let's try this—we are going to separate into two groups. Group 1 is going to start, and once they sing the first two lines, Group 2 will start from the beginning. Each group will sing it four times. Let's try it."

13. Reinforce: "Achieving important goals in our life that reflect our values, like friendships, start with setting the goal, identifying steps to take, and taking the first step. Once we have taken the first step, we take the next. Achieving goals can be very rewarding and help us create positive emotions."

14. Discussion questions:
    - Can you think of a time you set a goal to do something new and important to you?
    - When you achieved the goal, what were some emotions you had?
    - What are some goals you would like to achieve?
    - What are other important things in your life (i.e. values)?
    - What might be the first step?

✿ CUPS AND CLAPS

Module: Emotion Regulation

Skill addressed
Decreasing Vulnerabilities: Building Mastery

Summary
The main goal of this activity is to build mastery through learning a new rhythm and practicing it to improve.

Materials needed

- Recording of the song "Wellerman (Sea Shanty)" by Nathan Evans or "Cornbread and Butterbeans" by Carolina Chocolate Drops and means to play it
- Two plastic cups for each student

Lesson overview

1. Explain: "When we learn new things, we aren't perfect the first time. We get better each time we practice. This is called *building mastery.*"
2. Continue: "We are going to play a new rhythm today using two plastic cups. It might be tough at first, but we will get better each time."
3. Pass out two plastic cups to each student.
4. Teach the following pattern:
   - Take the right cup and put it on top of the left cup.
   - Clap three times.
   - Take the top cup off and place it back on the table.
   - Clap three times.
   - Take the left cup and place it on top of the right cup.
   - Clap three times.
   - Take the top cup off and place it back on the table.
   - Clap three times.
5. Practice one more time.
6. "This time, we are going to play our rhythm along to a song. Do your best to stay with the beat."
7. Repeat one more time.
8. Discussion questions:
   - What was easy about this activity?

- What was hard?
- How did you feel at the beginning?
- How did you feel once you were able to accomplish the movements?

Modifications for higher developmental level

1. Explain: "When we learn new things, we aren't perfect the first time. We get better each time we practice. This is called *building mastery.*"
2. Continue: "We are going to play a new rhythm today using two plastic cups. It might be tough at first, but we will get better each time."
3. Teach the following pattern:
   - Take the right cup and put it on top of the left cup.
   - Clap three times.
   - Take the top cup off and place it back on the table.
   - Clap three times.
   - Take the left cup and place it on top of the right cup.
   - Clap three times.
   - Take the top cup off and place it back on the table.
   - Take a cup in each hand, cross them, and place them back on the table in the opposite spot facing down.
   - Uncross your hands.
   - Turn each cup over at the same time and put them back on the table facing up.
   - Take a cup in each hand, cross them, and place back on the table in the opposite spot facing up.
   - Uncross your hands.
   - Turn each cup over at the same time and put them back on the table facing down.
   - Repeat instructions one more time.
   - Go back to the beginning and do it again!
4. "Now we will do it again, matching the beat of a song. Do your best. We will do it twice."
5. Discussion questions:
   - What was easy about this activity?
   - What was hard?
   - How did you feel at the beginning?
   - How did you feel once you were able to accomplish the movements?
   - Can you think of something that was hard for you at first, but you built mastery with practice?

❧ I THINK I CAN

Module: Emotion Regulation

Skill addressed
Decreasing Vulnerabilities: Cope Ahead

Summary
The main goal of this activity is to complete hard tasks through coping ahead.

Materials needed

- Book: *The Little Engine That Could*
- Adapted chant lyrics (included in lesson overview)
- List of physical challenges to complete (items for obstacle course if desired)
- List of tongue twisters
- List of possible coping skills for sadness and paper or whiteboard to write ideas if desired

Lesson overview

1. Explain: "Coping ahead means to get yourself prepared before you have to do something challenging. Sometimes we have to do things that are hard. For example, our bodies have to work hard, our minds have to work hard, or we experience an uncomfortable or hard emotion."
2. Explain: "Coping ahead is a way of encouraging yourself to do hard things by being prepared to face them."
3. Read the story of *The Little Engine That Could.*
4. Teach the children the chant using the following additional words: "I think I can, I think I can, I think I can with cope ahead."
5. Invite students to state the chant with you.
6. Choose one or more of the following physical activities for the children to complete. Share the directions and invite them to imagine themselves doing the task skillfully. Lead students in repeating the chant as they complete the physical activity.
   - Wall sit for 15 seconds then do 10 jumping jacks
   - Rub your head and pat your belly then switch
   - Lead children through an obstacle course set up in the room or on a playground

- Arm circles 10 times one way, 10 times the other way, then 10 arm raises

7. Choose one or more of the following tongue twister activities for the children to recite. Share the directions and invite them to imagine themselves doing the task skillfully. Lead the students in repeating the chant to prepare to complete the task.
   - "She sells seashells by the seashore"
   - "Peter Piper picked a peck of pickled peppers"
   - "Six slippery snails slid slowly seaward"
   - "Toy boat" (repeat many times)
   - "He threw three free throws"
   - "A happy hippo hopped and hiccupped"

8. Talk about the emotion sad: is it comfortable or uncomfortable? Talk about the emotion of feeling sad when there is no one to help. Give an example of a hypothetical scenario where they may feel sad in the future (e.g. not doing well on a school assignment). Ask students what coping skills they can use when feeling sad if they need help.

9. Possible coping skills:
   - Taking a deep breath
   - Finding a trusted adult to talk to
   - Asking a different friend to help
   - Write down or draw a picture of your emotions or the situation
   - Cry and hug a pillow, pet, or stuffed animal.

10. Have the students think of a time they were sad and a coping skill they could use if they feel this way again. Recite the chant.

11. Discussion questions:
    - Have you ever had to do something hard?
    - Do you think it would happen again if you could imagine yourself coping with it successfully?
    - Which activity was easy to complete?
    - Which activity was hard to complete?

Modifications for higher developmental level

1. Explain: "Coping ahead means to get yourself prepared before you have to do something challenging. Sometimes we have to do things that are hard. For example, our bodies have to work hard, our minds have to work hard, or we experience an uncomfortable or hard emotion."

2. Explain: "Coping ahead is a way of encouraging yourself to do hard things by being prepared to face them."

3. Have a student who remembers the story of *The Little Engine That Could* share. Read it if no one knows it.

4. Teach the children the chant using the following additional words: "I think I can, I think I can, I think I can with cope ahead."

5. Invite students to state the chant with you.

6. Choose one or more of the following physical activities for the children to complete. Share the directions and invite them to imagine themselves doing the task skillfully. Lead students in repeating the chant as they complete the physical activity. Have the students come up with some physical challenges or use the following:
   - Wall sit for 15 seconds then do 10 jumping jacks
   - Rub your head and pat your belly then switch
   - Lead children through an obstacle course set up in the room or on a playground
   - Arm circles 10 times one way, 10 times the other way, then 10 arm raises.

7. Choose two or more of the following tongue twister activities for the children to recite. Share the directions and invite them to imagine themselves doing the task skillfully. Lead the students in repeating the chant to prepare to complete the task.
   - "She sells seashells by the seashore"
   - "Peter Piper picked a peck of pickled peppers"
   - "Six slippery snails slid slowly seaward"
   - "Toy boat" (repeat many times)
   - "He threw three free throws"
   - "A happy hippo hopped and hiccupped"

8. Talk about the emotion sad: is it comfortable or uncomfortable? Talk about the emotion of feeling sad when there is no one to help. Give an example of a hypothetical scenario where they may feel sad in the future (e.g. not doing well on a school assignment). Ask students what coping skills they can use when feeling sad if they need help.

9. Possible coping skills:
   - Taking a deep breath
   - Finding a trusted adult to talk to
   - Asking a different friend to help
   - Write down or draw a picture of your emotions or the situation
   - Cry and hug a pillow, pet, or stuffed animal.

10. Have the students write out a time they were sad and a coping skill they could use if they feel this way again. Recite the chant. Have them identify two other uncomfortable emotions (e.g. angry or embarrassed), and complete the task for these emotions as well.

11. Discussion questions:
    - Ask if children have ever had to do something hard.
    - Ask if they think it would happen again if they can imagine themselves coping with it successfully.
    - Ask which activity was easy to complete.
    - Ask which activity was hard.

❀ I'M GOING ON A PICNIC

Module: Emotion Regulation

Skill addressed
Decreasing Vulnerabilities: PLEASE

Summary
The main goal of this activity is to help us understand the impact that eating, sleeping, exercise, and keeping ourselves well has on our emotions, through a fun chant.

Materials needed

♦ Whiteboard for writing out the chant
♦ Additional resources and handouts on healthy sleep tips, proper nutrition, avoiding drugs, and exercise

Lesson preparation

♦ Chant written on the board: "I'm going on a picnic and I'm going to bring..."
♦ Write on the board:
   ▪ PL: Physically welL
   ▪ E: Eat right
   ▪ A: Avoid drugs
   ▪ S: Sleep well
   ▪ E: Exercise
   Modify for younger children

Lesson overview

1. Ask: "What emotions do you feel when you are hungry? How about when you are tired? When you have a cold? When you have had too much sugar? Or how about when you are not allowed to run around and play?"
2. Say: "We can get stuck feeling angry, grumpy, and sad sometimes. Here are some ways to help keep that from happening. Let's create a chant to remember these important things. Let's start with healthy eating."
3. Introduce the chant: "I'm going on a picnic and I'm going to bring..."

4. Each student adds a healthy food. For a challenge start with A, B, C. For example, class chants: "I'm going on a picnic and I'm going to bring an apple, I'm going on a picnic and I'm going to bring a banana, etc."
5. Additional chants for physically well, sleeping well, and exercise are respectively: "I'm taking care of my body, and I'm going to do…," "I'm sleeping well tonight, so I'm going to…," and "I'm going to get some exercise, so a stretch I can do is…."
6. Ask: "What emotions do you feel when you take care of your body?"

Modifications for higher developmental level
MATERIALS NEEDED

♦ Additional resources and handouts on healthy sleep tips, proper nutrition, avoiding drugs, and exercise

LESSON PREPARATION

♦ Chant written on the board: "I'm going on a picnic and I'm going to bring…"
♦ Write on the board:
   ▪ PL: Treat physical illness
   ▪ E: Balanced eating
   ▪ A: Avoid mood-altering drugs
   ▪ S: Balance sleep
   ▪ E: Get exercise

LESSON OVERVIEW

1. Ask: "What emotions do you feel when you are hungry? How about when you are tired? When you have a cold? When you have had too much sugar? Or how about when you are not allowed to run around and play?"
2. Say: "We can get stuck feeling angry, grumpy, and sad sometimes. Here are some ways to help keep that from happening. Let's create a chant to remember these important things. Let's start with healthy eating."
3. Each student adds a healthy food. For a challenge start with A, B, C. For example, class chants: "I'm going on a picnic and I'm going to bring an apple, I'm going on a picnic and I'm going to bring a banana, etc." For an extra challenge, you can have the students try to remember all of the items said before them: "I'm going on a picnic and I'm going to bring an apple, a banana, carrots…."

4. Additional chants for physically well, sleeping well, and exercise are respectively: "I'm taking care of my body, and I'm going to do...," "I'm sleeping well tonight, so I'm going to...," and "I'm going to get some exercise, so a stretch I can do is...."

5. Ask: "What emotions do you feel when you take care of your body?"

6. Additional resources and handouts on healthy sleep tips, proper nutrition, avoiding drugs, and exercise can be utilized and reviewed.

✼ ABC SKILL REVIEW

Module: Emotion Regulation

Skill addressed
Decreasing Vulnerabilities: Accumulating positives, Building mastery, Cope ahead

Summary
The main goal of this activity is to review accumulating positives in the short term, building mastery, and cope ahead reminding us of ways one can manage difficult emotions through chant.

Materials needed
+ Blank paper, writing utensil (crayon, pencil, pen)
+ Chant that goes to the tune "ABC" by The Jackson Five

 Chorus:
 A B C, It's easy as 1,2,3
 We're building our mastery
 A,B,C, 1,2,3, come and learn with me.

 Chant:
 A, A, Accumulating Positives
 B, B, Building Mastery
 C, C, Cope Ahead

Lesson preparation

+ Write chant on the board

Lesson overview

1. Explain: "Today we are going to review three skills we have learned to prepare us to better face difficult feelings and situations. These skills can help us each separately or together to help us get ready for something hard."
2. Pass out three sheets of paper for each student.
3. "A stands for Accumulating Positives, which means doing fun things and

things that make you happy." Ask: "What is something that you think is fun and makes you feel good?"

4. Have students draw an A on the first sheet of paper.

5. "B stands for Building Mastery, which means practicing something over and over as you get better and better. This can help us feel proud of ourselves. One example is when babies learn to walk. They have to practice to get better, then they want to show everyone what they have learned." Ask: "What was something you had to practice and, as you got better at it, you felt happier and prouder?"

6. Have the students draw a B on the second sheet of paper.

7. "C stands for Cope Ahead, which means preparing to get through something coming up that may be hard." Ask: "Have you ever had to tell yourself, 'I can do this!'?"

8. Have the students draw a C on the third sheet.

9. Teach the ABC Skills chant.

10. Divide the students into three groups.

11. Assign each group a different letter, A, B, or C.

12. Have the students hold up the letter they were assigned when their letter is mentioned in the chant.

13. Encourage the students to join in singing the chorus and chant.

Modifications for higher developmental level

1. Explain: "Today we are going to review three skills we have learned to prepare us to better face difficult feelings and situations. These skills can help us each separately or together to help us get ready for something hard."

2. Pass out three sheets of paper for each student.

3. "A stands for Accumulating Positives, which means doing fun things and things that make you happy." Ask: "What is something that you think is fun and makes you feel good?"

4. Have students draw an A on the first sheet of paper.

5. "B stands for Building Mastery, which means practicing something over and over as you get better and better. This can help us feel proud of ourselves. One example is when babies learn to walk. They have to practice to get better, then they want to show everyone what they have learned." Ask: "What was something you had to practice and, as you got better at it, you felt happier and prouder?"

6. Have the students draw a B on the second sheet of paper.

7. "C stands for Cope Ahead, which means preparing to get through something coming up that may be hard." Ask: "Have you ever had to tell yourself, 'I can do this!'?"

8. Have the students draw a C on the third sheet.

9. Teach the ABC Skills chant.

10. Have the students stand up and add movements to the song by using their bodies to make the letters, A, B, C.

11. Encourage students to take turns sharing answers from their papers. Sing chant, share "A" answers. Sing chant, share "B" answers. And lastly, sing chant, share "C" answers. End with chant.

✿ RIDE THE WAVE

Module: Emotion Regulation

Skill addressed
Managing Really Hard Emotions: The Wave Skill—Mindfulness of Current Emotions

Summary
The main goal of this activity is to learn to ride out an emotion like a wave versus distracting ourselves/pushing away an emotion or holding onto it.

Materials needed

+ Song about surfing
+ "Surfin' USA" by The Beach Boys (Karaoke Track)
+ Lyrics of "Ride the Wave" song (included in lesson overview)

Lesson overview

1. Ask: "What emotions do you wish would last forever? What emotions do you wish would go away quickly?" Explain: "Emotions come and go, like waves in the ocean. Some are bigger than others, some are smaller."
2. Have the students stand up and imagine riding a surfboard over small waves and then over large waves.
3. Explain: "All emotions are important. Even the ones that are uncomfortable! It is important to notice the waves and stay on the surfboard so we can learn to ride the waves, instead of getting pummelled by them."
4. Sing or read the following to the tune of "Surfin' USA":

Verse 1:
Making friends with our emotions
We feel them like a wave
Knowing our emotions
Will help us through the day
Sometimes great big emotions
Can feel like just too much
That's when we step back and do the emotion wave.

Chorus:
We can surf our emotions
Surf our emotion waves
Let's all try together, to do the emotion wave.
If we picture our emotions coming in and out.
That's how we can handle our emotion waves.

Verse 2:
One day I hit my brother.
He had called me a name
I was feeling very mad and my fists got really tight
If I surfed my emotions, instead of lashing out
the feeling would have passed
Without a doubt

Repeat the chorus

5. Have the students stand up and ride the waves as they listen to the song/ chant again. Ask them to shout out emotions that are big for them and then emotions that are small. There are no right or wrong answers.
6. Explain: "All emotions teach us about ourselves and our world; if we can slow down and ride them out, it helps us make helpful choices in how to respond to them."

Modifications for higher developmental level

1. Ask: "What emotions do you wish would last forever? What emotions do you wish would go away quickly?" Explain: "Emotions come and go, like waves in the ocean. Some are bigger than others, some are smaller."
2. Have the students stand up and imagine riding a surfboard over small waves and then over large waves.
3. Explain: "All emotions are important. Even the ones that are uncomfortable! It is important to notice the waves and stay on the surfboard so we can learn to ride the waves, instead of getting pummelled by them."
4. Pass out the words to the song. Sing or read the following to the tune of "Surfin' USA":

Verse 1:
Making friends with our emotions
We feel them like a wave
Knowing our emotions
Will help us through the day
Sometimes great big emotions
Can feel like just too much
That's when we step back and do the emotion wave.

Chorus:
We can surf our emotions
Surf our emotion waves
Let's all try together, to do the emotion wave.
If we picture our emotions coming in and out.
That's how we can handle our emotion waves.

Verse 2:
One day I hit my brother.
He had called me a name
I was feeling very mad and my fists got really tight
If I surfed my emotions, instead of lashing out
the feeling would have passed
Without a doubt

Repeat the chorus

5. Have the students stand up and ride the waves as they listen to the song/ chant again. Ask them to shout out emotions that are big for them and then emotions that are small. There are no right or wrong answers.
6. Explain: "All emotions teach us about ourselves and our world; if we can slow down and ride them out, it helps us make helpful choices in how to respond to them."
7. Have the students read the second verse and share experiences in which they acted on big emotions instead of riding the wave.
8. Have the students repeat the chorus while surfing on an imaginary surfboard.

INTERPERSONAL EFFECTIVENESS

Interpersonal effectiveness skills encourage the development of the ability to ask for what one needs, saying no, maintaining relationships, and preserving one's self-respect in helpful, and not hurtful, ways. Sometimes people can fall into a more passive style of communicating (e.g. not speaking up for themselves or asking for what they want at all), or a more aggressive style (e.g. demanding what they want, raising their voice). Interpersonal effectiveness skills aim to help us find balance to fall somewhere on that spectrum that will get us the best outcomes for the situation we're facing. Teaching safe, effective ways to communicate is a core goal of this module. Traditional assertiveness techniques are strengthened by learning to reflect on what the priorities are in any given interaction, determining what it is that I am asking for, and figuring out how to say it in the most effective way. These skills allow us to express ourselves clearly and strengthen our relationship with others and ourselves.

Skills addressed in this module include:

- Identifying objectives—what am I asking for?
- DEAR MAN formula to ask for what you want or say no in an effective way
- GIVE—how to ask to keep or strengthen the relationship
- FAST—how to ask to keep self-respect.

Elements of the skills will be found in the lessons in this section. These skills can be taught separately or in combination.

Here are the formulas for the skills listed, as found in Linehan's *DBT Skills Training Manual* (2015).

DEAR MAN

D: Describe the Situation
E: Express Emotion and Opinion
A: Assert What Is Wanted/Needed
R: Reinforce Gains for Self/Other
M: Stay Mindful
A: Act Confident
N: Negotiate

GIVE

G: Be Gentle
I: Act Interested
V: Validate
E: Use an Easy Manner

FAST

F: Be Fair
A: No Over-Apologizing
S: Stick to Your Values
T: Be Truthful

❧ DEAR MAN TO ASK FOR WHAT YOU WANT

Module: Interpersonal Effectiveness

Skill addressed
DEAR MAN Skill (entire skill)

Summary
The main goal of this activity is to learn the formula for asking for what you want or saying no in a way that will increase your chances of getting what you're asking for.

Materials needed

- Recording of the DEAR MAN song and a means to play it (recording available at https://www.youtube.com/playlist?list=PL0jguhoPs0m6qrlh hTR7P4PPtz7wuicy1 or by scanning the QR code in the Appendix)
- Lyrics to the song (see lyrics at the end of this exercise, you can also download a copy to print from www.jkp.com/catalogue/book/9781805013211)

Lesson overview

1. Listen to the song.
2. Select a scenario from those listed below; for example: You want to play a different game than your friend. Replay the song and stop after each letter.
3. Describe—have the class describe the facts of the scenario.
4. Then replay the song. Stop at E: Express. Have the class identify emotions one might have in this scenario.
5. Replay the song. Assert. Have the class share what they want from their friend in this scenario.
6. Replay the song. Reinforce. Have the class identify why your request is important to both you and your friend.
7. Replay the song. Be Mindful. Have the class identify the goal.
8. Replay the song. Act Confident. Have the class share confident ways to ask their friend.
9. Replay the song. Negotiate. Ask the students to come up with compromises in this scenario.

Modifications for higher developmental level

1. Have students pair up in teams and select scenarios to role play.
2. Display the lyrics.
3. Play the song and ask the students to join in singing as they catch on.
4. After singing the song, as a group write out a DEAR MAN for a scenario such as:
   - You want to play a different game than your friend
   - Your mom doesn't want to drive you to your friend's house
   - Or choose a character from a movie or a book and write a DEAR MAN on that character's behalf.
5. Discussion questions:
   - Can you think of a time that you might use this? Or that you wished you had used this?
   - How do you think it might help you?

DEAR MAN Song

By Deborah Spiegel MT-BC copyright 2010

DEAR MAN DEAR MAN to ask for what you want,
use DEAR MAN DEAR MAN to ask for what you want.

D- Describe the current situation (x3)
When you ask for what you want.

Let's sum it all up now,
D-
Describe the current situation
Dear man Dear man to ask for what you want.

E- Express your feelings and opinions (x3)
When you ask for what you want

Let's sum it all up now,
D and E
D- Describe the current situation
E- Express your feelings and opinions
Dear man Dear man to ask for what you want.

A- Assert by asking or say no (x3)
When you ask for what you want

Let's sum it all up now,
D- E and A
D- Describe the current situation
E- Express your feelings and opinions
A- Assert by asking or say no
Dear man Dear man to ask for what you want.

R- Reinforce the person you are asking (x3)
When you ask for what you want

Let's sum it all up now,
D- E -A and R
D- Describe the current situation

E- Express your feelings and opinions
A- Assert by asking or say no
R- Reinforce the person you are asking
Dear man Dear man to ask for what you want.

M- Be mindful, stay focused on your goal (x3)
When you ask for what you want

Let's sum it all up now,
D- E -A-R-M
D- Describe the current situation
E- Express your feelings and opinions
A- Assert by asking or say no
R- Reinforce the person you are asking
M- Be mindful, stay focused on your goal
Dear man Dear man to ask for what you want.

A- Appear like you feel confident (x3)
When you ask for what you want

Let's sum it all up now,
D- E -A-R-M and A
D- Describe the current situation
E- Express your feelings and opinions
A- Assert by asking or say no
R- Reinforce the person you are asking
M- Be mindful, stay focused on your goal
A- Appear like you feel confident
Dear man Dear man to ask for what you want.

N- Negotiate for other options (x3)
When you ask for what you want

Let's sum it all up now,
D- E -A-R-M -A-N
D- Describe the current situation
E- Express your feelings and opinions
A- Assert by asking or say no
R- Reinforce the person you are asking

M- Be mindful, stay focused on your goal
A- Appear like you feel confident
N- Negotiate for other options
Dear man Dear man to ask for what you want.

Again (can repeat the last summary)

See lyrics for sharing with students:

D- Describe the current situation
E- Express your feelings and opinions
A- Assert by asking or say no
R- Reinforce the person you are asking
M- Be mindful, stay focused on your goal
A- Appear like you feel confident
N- Negotiate for other options

❀ DESCRIBE

Module: Interpersonal Effectiveness

Skill addressed
DEAR MAN: Describe

Summary
The main goal of this activity is to learn to describe without judgment or opinion. The first step in the DEAR MAN formula.

Materials needed
- Recorded music and the means to play it
- Drawing materials

Lesson overview

1. Teach the following lyrics to the melody of Twinkle Twinkle Little Star:

   Describe what happened, what do you see?
   A bird? Did it fly? Or land in a tree?
   Use your words, keep it true
   What did you see? Let us hear from you.
   Describe what happened, what do you see?
   A bird? Did it fly? Or land in a tree?

2. Talk with the students about describing. "Today we will practice describing things, just using the facts, just what you observe."
3. "For example, tell me what you notice." (Hold up a pencil and drop it on the desk.) "How would you describe that?" (E.g. "The teacher held a yellow pencil while she was talking and she dropped the pencil on the desk and then it rolled over and touched her cup.")
4. Practice several other actions using objects in the classroom and ask the students to describe what they observe. Sing the song in between each action.
   - Possible scenarios: Close a door, roll a ball, kick the trash can over, jump up and down and laugh...
5. Invite students to draw a picture of something they see in the room. Encourage them to describe their drawings to the class.

6. After this, sing the "D- Describe the current situation" section of the DEAR MAN song.

Modifications for higher developmental level
MATERIALS NEEDED

◆ A way for students to hear/listen to songs
◆ Drawing materials
◆ Two different versions of the song "Lean on Me"—one sung by Bill Withers (the original version) and the version sung by the cast from the television show Glee

LESSON OVERVIEW

1. Talk with the students about describing. "Today we will practice describing things, just using the facts, just what you observe."
2. "For example, tell me what you notice." (Hold up a pencil and drop it on the desk.) "How would you describe that?" (E.g. "The teacher held a yellow pencil while she was talking and she dropped the pencil on the desk and then it rolled over and touched her cup.")
3. Practice several other actions using objects in the classroom and ask the students to describe what they observe. Sing the song in between each action.
   ▪ Possible scenarios: Close a door, roll a ball, kick the trash can over, jump up and down and laugh...
4. Invite students to draw a picture of something they see in the room. Encourage them to describe their drawings to the class.
5. Play the two versions of "Lean on Me"—the original and the Glee version.
   ▪ After each song, have children practice describing using just the facts, no judgments or opinions (leave out saying if you like or don't like it).
   ▪ After they have heard both of the versions of the song, describe what they notice is the same and different.
6. After this, sing the "D- Describe the current situation" section of the DEAR MAN song.
7. Discussion questions:
   ▪ Was it hard to describe with just the facts, leaving out opinions and judgments?
   ▪ Describing is the first step in DEAR MAN, a formula for asking for what you want in a way that will make you more likely to get what you're asking for. Why would it be helpful to describe the situation?

✿ STOP, FRIEND!

Module: Interpersonal Effectiveness

Skill addressed
DEAR MAN: Express Feelings and Assert/Ask

Summary
The main goal of this activity is to learn ways to express our emotions using words and practice assertiveness through a song and scenarios.

Materials needed

◆ Chant/Song lyrics

Lesson preparation

◆ Write the chant/lyrics on the board
◆ Learn the American Sign Language (ASL) Sign for Stop[1]
◆ Learn the ASL Sign for Safe
◆ Learn the chant:
   Start by chanting this verse while patting and clapping the beat

   (Comma indicates a pause, or a breath)
   I use,
   my words,
   to tell you how I feel.
   I use,
   my words,
   to tell you how I feel.
   I use,
   my words,
   to tell you how I feel.
   I use,
   my words,
   to tell you how I feel.

---

1   If you are working outside of the US, substitute the appropriate signs from your local language, such as British Sign Language (BSL) or Auslan sign language of the Australian deaf community

Scenario: What if a friend isn't keeping you safe?
Then you say...

Chorus: (To the tune of the folk song Shoo Fly, Don't Bother Me)
Stop, Friend! (American Sign Language (ASL) sign for Stop)
Please keep me safe (ASL sign for Safe)
Stop, Friend! (ASL sign for Stop)
Please keep me safe (ASL sign for Safe)
Stop, Friend! (ASL sign for Stop)
Please keep me safe (ASL sign for Safe)
Please be kind and keep me safe. (Make a heart with hands)

I use,
my words,
to tell you how I feel.
I use,
my words,
to tell you how I feel.
I use,
my words,
to tell you how I feel.
I use,
my words,
to tell you how I feel.

Scenario: What if a friend is too loud?

Chorus: (To the tune of Shoo Fly, Don't Bother Me)
Stop, Friend! (ASL sign for Stop)
You're too loud (ASL sign for Safe)
Stop, Friend! (ASL sign for Stop)
You're too loud (ASL sign for Safe)
Stop, Friend! (ASL sign for Stop)
You're too loud (ASL sign for Safe)
Please be kind and talk softly. (Make a heart with hands)

I use,
my words,
to tell you how I feel.

I use,
my words,
to tell you how I feel.
I use,
my words,
to tell you how I feel.
I use,
my words,
to tell you how I feel.

Scenario: What if a friend is too close?

Chorus: (To the tune of Shoo Fly, Don't Bother Me)
Stop, Friend! (ASL sign for Stop)
You're too loud (ASL sign for Safe)
Stop, Friend! (ASL sign for Stop)
You're too loud (ASL sign for Safe)
Stop, Friend! (ASL sign for Stop)
You're too close (ASL sign for Safe)
Please be kind and give me space. (Make a heart with hands)

Lesson overview

1. Teach the ASL Stop and Safe Signs to students.
2. Teach the chorus of the song to students.
3. Teach the chanted verse of the song while maintaining a steady beat by patting and clapping.
4. Explain to students that it is important to use our words to say how we feel. "When we use our words, then friends, teachers, and family can better understand and know what to do/how to help."
5. Practice chant/song with movements. Between the chant and the chorus, give a scenario (e.g. What if a friend is not keeping you safe, or What if a friend is too close?).
6. Have students get into partners to do a patty-cake type movement during chant, then practice telling each other the chorus.
7. Discussion questions:
   - What was it like to tell your friend to stop? Was it easy? Hard?
   - If a friend still doesn't stop after you asked them to, what should we do next? (Get an adult)

8. Sing the DEAR MAN song through D-E and A.

Modifications for higher developmental level

1. Replace the chant with a song such as "Roar" by Katy Perry, or "Brave" by Sara Bareilles.
2. Have the lyrics posted on a whiteboard or smart screen for everyone to see.
3. Discuss the lyrics.
4. Ask the students:
   - "Is it difficult to tell someone how you feel sometimes?"
   - "What do you think would happen if you say what you want to say?"
5. "Let's learn a helpful way to say what you want to say so you don't hurt your friend's feelings, or feel embarrassed" (or whatever they say they are worried about).
6. Give a social scenario to students (e.g. Your friend said something that hurt your feelings, or a friend didn't include you at recess, etc.).
7. Have students use the "I" message approach:
   - I feel...
   - When you...
   - So can you please...
8. Challenge the students to come up with possible social scenarios.
9. Discussion questions:
   - What was it like to use your words in this way? Easy? Hard?
   - Why is it important to say how we feel and use words to express our needs?
   - When you use I statements, is it easier?
10. Sing the DEAR MAN song through D-E and A.

❀ REINFORCE! THANK YOU

Module: Interpersonal Effectiveness

Skill addressed
DEAR MAN: Reinforce

Summary
The main goal of this activity is to practice sharing gratitude and "reinforcing" the person you're asking, letting them know what's in it for them to grant you what you are requesting.

Materials needed

- A song about expressing gratitude and the means to play it (e.g. "Thank You" by Brandin Reed; "Thank You for Being a Friend" by Andrew Gold; "Thanks a Lot" by Raffi; "Thankful" by Josh Groban
- Blank thank you notes or construction paper or white paper
- Markers, crayons, colored pencils

Lesson preparation

- Cue audio
- Offer a variety of paper and writing materials or blank thank you cards for students to write on

Lesson overview

1. Explain that in the DEAR MAN skill the R stands for reinforce. This can mean sharing with the other person how what you are asking for can benefit them. It could be expressing thankfulness to that person.
   - I would be thankful if (they give you what you are asking for or do what you are asking them to do)
   - I would be thankful if we could take turns with the ball
   - I would be thankful if I could finish watching this TV show.
   - I would be thankful if we could play tag and then play the game you wish to play.
2. Ask: "What are some things you want to ask another person for?"
3. "How could you say thank you for that?"

4. Invite the students to draw or write on the thank you card. Play the song you have chosen as they work.

5. Sing the whole DEAR MAN song.

Modifications for higher developmental level

1. Explain that in the DEAR MAN skill the R stands for reinforce. This can mean sharing with the other person how what you are asking for can benefit them. It could be expressing thankfulness to that person.
   - I would be thankful if (they give you what you are asking for or do what you are asking them to do).
   - I would be thankful if we could take turns with the ball.
   - I would be thankful if I could finish watching this TV show.
   - I would be thankful if we could play tag and then play the game you wish to play.

2. Ask: "What are some things you want to ask another person for?"

3. "How could you say thank you for that?"

4. Invite the students to draw or write on the thank you card. Play the song you have chosen as they work.

5. Discussion questions:
   - When someone has said thank you to you, does it reinforce wanting to be helpful again?
   - When someone is kind to you, does it make you want to do what they ask?
   - Is there anything you've wanted to ask for recently? Do you think saying thank you would help you get what you want?
   - Has anyone ever said thank you to you when you were kind to them? How did that feel?
   - Can you think of something you want to ask for and how you could thank/reinforce the person you are asking?
   - What are other ways besides a card that you can say thank you?

6. Sing the whole DEAR MAN song.

G IS FOR GENTLE

Module: Interpersonal Effectiveness

Skill addressed

GIVE: Be Gentle

Summary

The main goal of this activity is to find ways to be gentle when communicating.

Materials needed

- Song lyrics to "I Like Little Kitty." These can be read like a poem or sung as a song. "I Like Little Kitty" was originally written by Jane Taylor and is in the public domain and easily available. The lyrics are modified to fit this skill lesson
- Means to play the song if you use a recorded version
- Stuffed animal or doll. Invite children to bring one from home for this day if you don't have these available

Lesson preparation

- Ensure that each student has a stuffed animal or doll to use
- Cue up music if you choose to use a recorded version for the first verse of the song

Lesson overview

1. Ask: "What does it mean to be gentle?"
2. Listen to this song/poem and show me how to be gentle with your stuffed animal. During verse one, take your stuffed animal, doll, or other toy and pretend it's a kitty you can pet. During the second verse, pretend your stuffed animal, doll, or toy is a friend. Be physically gentle with a stuffed animal and talk to him/her gently.
3. Read or play the song:

   I Like Little Kitty

   By Jane Taylor (verse 1) and modified by authors of this book (verse 2)

   I like little kitty,
   Her coat is so warm;

And if I don't hurt her
She'll do me no harm.
So I'll not pull her tail,
Nor drive her away,
But Kitty and I
Very gently will play.

When I talk to my friends
I'll use gentle words.
I'll talk very calmly
I can hear and be heard.
So I'll not say mean things
Nor yell, scream, or shout.
My friends and I
Very gently hang out.

4. Discussion questions:
   - How does it make us feel when we are gentle with others?
   - How does it make you feel when people are gentle with you?
   - How does it feel when others are harsh with us?

Modifications for higher developmental level
MATERIALS NEEDED

- Song lyrics on respect (included in lesson preparation)

LESSON PREPARATION

- Write out the song lyrics for all students to see:
  RESPECT find out what it means to me
  RESPECT gentle is the way to be

LESSON OVERVIEW

1. Ask: "What does it mean to be gentle?"
2. Prompt discussion with the students about gentleness in the words that you choose to use.
3. Ask if gentleness can be demonstrated with your actions. With your attitude?

4. Explain that acting in a way that is gentle is similar to acting with respect.
5. Explain that today we are going to practice being gentle.
6. Demonstrate the following chant for the students. This can be chanted or sung to the tune of the song "RESPECT" by Aretha Franklin.
   RESPECT find out what it means to me
   RESPECT gentle is the way to be
7. Invite students to partner up. Each partner will take a turn asking something of their partner in a gentle manner.
8. Sing the chant as a group and then pause. During this time one partner will practice asking in a gentle manner. Sing the chant a second time as an entire group, then pause. During this pause the second partner will take a turn asking in a gentle manner.
9. Discussion questions:
   - How does it make us feel when we are gentle with others?
   - How does it make you feel when people are gentle with you?
   - How does it feel when others are harsh with us?
   - When is it hard to be gentle/respectful?
   - When is it easy to be gentle/respectful?

✿ ACT INTERESTED

Module: Interpersonal Effectiveness

Skill addressed
GIVE: (Act) Interested

Summary
The main goal of this activity is to demonstrate acting interested as one practices being a good listener.

Materials needed

- Lyrics for the song about good listening (included in the lesson overview, recording available at https://www.youtube.com/playlist?list=PL0 jguhoPs0m6qrlhhTR7P4PPtz7wuicy1 or by scanning the QR code in the Appendix)
- Optional: a recording of the song "Sailing, Sailing" by Godfrey Marks and means to play the recording

Lesson preparation

- Be prepared to sing the song with the students
- Cue audio if using

Lesson overview

1. Explain: "Showing that you are interested in hearing what another person has to say can help you keep a good relationship with that person." This is important when talking with a friend, a teacher, or a parent or another adult.
2. "We can show we are interested in someone by what our body does while we listen to them. Today we are going to learn a song to practice good listening with our body."
3. Use the audio to listen or sing the following song for the students to the tune of the 1880 song "Sailing, Sailing" written by Godfrey Marks:

   Listening, listening; show interest in what you say.
   open eyes, turn toward you, be quiet, and use my ears

Listening, listening; show interest in what you say.
Wait to talk until I hear just what you say.

4. Invite students to sing the song along with you.
5. Teach movements with the body parts named as follows:
   - "Open eyes": point to your eyes
   - "Turn toward you": turn body
   - "Be quiet": point to mouth
   - "Use my ears": point to ears.
6. Discussion questions:
   - What are three ways you can show someone you are interested in listening to them?
   - Who can you listen to with these good listening skills?
   - When is the next time you can practice acting interested with good listening?
   - What is easy about listening well?
   - What is hard about listening well?

Modifications for higher developmental level
MATERIALS NEEDED

- A recording and the means to play it; song choices could include: "Listen" by Beyoncé Knowles; "I'm Listening ft. Hollyn" by Chris McClarney; "I Hear You" by Vicetone

LESSON PREPARATION

- Choose a song and cue audio

LESSON OVERVIEW

1. Ask students to share what good listening skills look like.
2. Invite them to share ideas to create a list of actions to take to demonstrate good listening (don't interrupt, look toward the person, turn your body toward the person, keep a calm body, avoid making faces or rolling eyes).
3. Invite students to partner up and practice poor and then good listening skills.
4. Play a song similar to one of the choices listed above and listen. Then invite students to practice good listening skills while they share what they heard in the song.

5. Discussion questions:
   - What are three ways you can show someone you are interested in listening to them?
   - Who can you listen to with these good listening skills?
   - When is the next time you can practice acting interested with good listening?
   - What is easy about listening well?
   - What is hard about listening well?

ACTIVE LISTENING!

Module: Interpersonal Effectiveness

Skill addressed

GIVE: Validation

Summary

The main goal of this activity is to learn how to validate through reflective listening.

Materials needed

- A written list of phrases that the students can use to clap syllables
- Optional pictures to pair with each of the phrases

Lesson preparation

- Prepare a list of phrases. Depending on your group it may help to limit the choices to a maximum of four. Options could include the following:
  - I like spaghetti
  - Peanut butter sandwich
  - Green beans
  - See ya later, alligator
  - Cheese pizza
  - I like to sing
  - I like the color red
  - I love to read
  - I don't like corn
- Prepare pictures to pair with each of the phrases

Lesson overview

1. Explain: "One way to practice validation is to reflect back what it is that you heard another person saying to you. This means it is important to listen to others and hear what they have to say."
2. Instruct: "Today we are going to practice paying attention to what someone says. We are going to do this by clapping rhythms back and forth."
3. Invite the students to use their name and clap the rhythm of the syllables.

Give an example using your own name clapping with the syllables you verbalize. (E.g. "Mrs. Jones" and clap with each syllable.)

4. Pause and invite the students to clap your name back repeating what you did.

5. Invite each of the students to stand up one at a time and clap their name. After the student claps with the name, then point to the remaining students in the group to clap and say the rhythm of the name back. (E.g. Student 1: "Maria" clap with each syllable; Remaining students respond back "Maria" while clapping with syllables.)

6. Repeat for each student.

7. Present the list you created of optional phrases. Invite each student to pick their favorite phrase and clap the rhythm of the phrase for the remaining students to repeat back.

8. Discussion questions:
   - What did you think when the remaining students repeated your name back? How did it make you feel?
   - What did you think when the remaining students repeated your favorite phrase back? How did it make you feel?
   - What was easy about validating (or use the term "hearing") your classmate?
   - What was hard about validating your classmate?
   - When someone talks to you, is it hard or easy to listen and hear what they say?

Modifications for higher developmental level

1. Explain: "One way to practice validation is to reflect back what it is that you heard another person saying to you. This means it is important to listen to others and hear what they have to say."

2. Instruct: "Today we are going to practice paying attention to what someone says. We are going to do this by clapping rhythms back and forth."

3. Invite the students to use their name and clap the rhythm of the syllables. Give an example using your own name clapping with the syllables you verbalize. (E.g. "Mrs. Jones" and clap with each syllable.)

4. Pause and invite the students to clap your name back repeating what you did.

5. Invite each of the students to stand up one at a time and clap their name. After the student claps with the name, then point to the remaining students in the group to clap and say the rhythm of the name back. (E.g.

Student 1: "Maria" clap with each syllable; Remaining students respond back "Maria" while clapping with syllables.)

6. Repeat for each student.
7. Provide a longer list of possible phrases to choose from.
8. Pair students with a partner.
9. Give these partner pairs the opportunity to clap rhythms of phrases back and forth with one another.
10. Invite partners to present a list of three of the options to the second partner (pictures could be used here) and clap the rhythm without the verbal words. Have the second partner guess from the clapping which phrase the first partner was presenting.
11. Discussion questions:
    - Can you think of a time when someone validated what you said or the way you felt? How did you feel when they listened to you?
    - Can you think of a time when someone did not listen well to you? How did you feel?
    - Next time you are listening to someone talk, how can you use this skill?

✼ EASY EXPRESSIONS

Module: Interpersonal Effectiveness

Skill addressed
GIVE: (Use an) Easy Manner

Summary
The main goal of this activity is to learn ways our voice can help us achieve goals through using an easy manner.

Lesson overview

1. Explain: "We are going to explore different ways to use our voice today. Listen and say after me" (call and response):

   Teacher: "This is my speaking voice." (stated in a normal speaking voice)
   Students: "This is my speaking voice."
   Teacher: "This is my shouting voice." (stated in a loud shouting voice)
   Students: "This is my shouting voice."
   Teacher: "This is my quiet voice." (stated in a quiet voice)
   Students: "This is my quiet voice."
   Teacher: "This is my whisper voice." (stated in a whisper)
   Students: "This is my whisper voice."
   Teacher: "This is my robot voice." (stated robotically)
   Students: "This is my robot voice."
   Teacher: "This is my singing voice." (singing)
   Students: "This is my singing voice."

2. Ask:
   - When is it best to use your regular talking voice?
   - When is it best to use your shouting voice?
   - When is it best to use your quiet voice?
   - When is it best to use your whisper voice?
   - When is it best to use your robot voice?
   - When is it best to use your singing voice?
   - What kind of voice is most helpful when asking a friend or grown-up for something that you want?

3. Do another round of call and response.

Teacher: "This is my calm and easy voice." (stated in a calm and easy manner)
Students: "This is my calm and easy voice."
Teacher: "This is my loud and harsh voice." (stated in a loud and harsh manner)
Students: "This is my loud and harsh voice."
Teacher: "This is my whiny voice." (stated in a whiny manner)
Students: "This is my whiny voice."
Repeat to emphasize the desired and ideal tone and manner:
Teacher: "This is my calm and easy voice." (stated in a calm and easy manner)
Students: "This is my calm and easy voice."

4. Ask: "Which voice works the best for asking for what you want?"
5. Have students practice using a calm and easy voice to ask a friend to share or asking to use something (such as a crayon, or toy, etc.).

Modifications for higher developmental level
MATERIALS NEEDED

♦ If available, percussion instruments such as drums or rhythm sticks; if not available, use body percussion
♦ Devise a list of questions that one student might want to ask a peer or friend (e.g. Can I borrow a pencil? Do you want to play at recess? Will you please move?, etc.)

LESSON PREPARATION

♦ Write questions on note cards or slips of paper to be read aloud by the teacher (e.g. May I borrow your pencil? May I read your book when you are done?)

LESSON OVERVIEW

1. Have students come up with a list of all the different ways we use our voice and list them on the whiteboard or smartboard. (E.g. loud, quiet, whisper, sarcastic, aggressive, etc.)
2. Have students come up with a list of musical elements and list them in a

separate list on the whiteboard or smartboard. (E.g. fast, slow, loud, soft, short, long, emphasized (accented), etc.)

3. Ask: "Have you ever heard the saying 'It's not what you say, it's how you say it?' Do you think that that's true or false? Why?"

4. Introduce activity: "We're going to use body percussion today to explore the different ways we could ask for what we want."

5. Activity:
   a. Have students get into pairs.
   b. The teacher will pick from a list of questions that one peer might say to another—they will read it aloud.
   c. One person is the listener—the listener chooses a voice choice and a musical element from the lists on the whiteboard or smartboard.
   d. The other person is the asker—they "ask" for something using body percussion (stomping feet, clapping, snapping, etc.) using the elements chosen by the listener. Then they ask that same question using their words in those same elements.
   e. Each student takes turns being the listener and the asker.

6. Discussion questions:
   - When you were the asker, what elements felt easy, what felt hard?
   - When you were the listener, what elements felt easy to listen to? What felt hard to listen to?
   - Which elements (manners) helped you feel open, calm, and ready to say "Yes" to the ask? Which elements made you feel like you wanted to say "No" to the ask?
   - What body language did you use when you were the asker? How? What body language did you notice from the listener when you asked in the different styles?

✿ FAST FRIENDS

Module: Interpersonal Effectiveness

Skill addressed
FAST

Summary
The main goal is to learn to use the qualities of the FAST skill to feel good about yourself so that you can in turn be both true to yourself, and be a better friend.

Materials needed

*   Recording of "FAST Friends" song and means to play it (recording available at https://www.youtube.com/playlist?list=PL0jguhoPs0m6qrlhh TR7P4PPtz7wuicy1 or by scanning the QR code in the Appendix)

Lesson preparation

*   Practice the song or be prepared to play the recording

Lesson overview

1. Ask the student(s) to list all the qualities of being a good friend (nice, fun, share toys, etc.).
2. Invite student(s) to listen to the song "FAST Friends" and begin singing along to the chorus as they learn it.
3. Lead a discussion with the students about what each part of the word FAST stands for and what it means.
    *   F—Fair: be fair to yourself and the other person / difference between needs and wants
    *   A—Apologies: don't over (or under) apologize / you don't have to apologize for who you are or how you feel but you should apologize if you make a mistake
    *   S—Stick to your values: use your wise mind skills and make choices that are right for you and support your values
    *   T—be Truthful: do not lie, act helpless, or exaggerate the truth
4. Make the song interactive. Add body percussion to the following words

and have the students perform the sound/motion when they hear the special word. (Only during the word)

- "FAST" (example: I want to be a FAST friend)—everyone/fast feet
- "Fair"—clap
- "Apologize"—pat legs
- "Stick"—tap fingers
- "Truthful/Truth"—rub hands together

Modifications for higher developmental level
MATERIALS NEEDED

- Spoons—one less than the number of students playing the game (see modification for groups of fewer than three students)
- Printable scenario/game cards (see the end of the activity, you can also download a copy to print from www.jkp.com/catalogue/book/9781805013211)

LESSON PREPARATION

- Arrange spoons in a circle in the center of your playing area (within reach of the students)
- Print scenario/game cards

LESSON OVERVIEW

1. Present the game scenarios (see game cards on the next page) and invite the students to play a game of FAST Friends. The rules are:
   a. Read each scenario and decide if the action on the card is a FAST skill or not. If it isn't a FAST skill, you'll reach out and grab a spoon as *fast* as you can.
   b. If the scenario is a FAST skill, have the students identify which part of the skill it represents.
   c. If the scenario is not a FAST skill, after the group reaches out and grabs spoons, have the one that did not get a spoon quickly enough describe how the scenario could have been different to make it a FAST skill.
   d. After the discussion, replace the spoons and play again with a new card.

MODIFICATION FOR SMALL GROUP OR INDIVIDUAL PLAY

◆ Instead of playing the "spoons" style game, you can invite the students to role play the scenarios and then decide if it meets the FAST skill or not. If they determine the scenario meets the FAST skill, ask them which letter is represented (F.A.S.T.). If they determine the scenario did not meet the FAST skill, have them recreate the role play correcting the problem and making it right.

FAST Friends Game Cards

You and a classmate are playing a game and won't give you a turn.	Your mom asks if you made your bed before school and you say "yes," but you really didn't.	You share your cookies with a friend at lunch.	Dad asks if you cleaned your room and you honestly tell him, "no sir, not yet."
A student in your class tells you, "if you are really my friend, you'll go pull that girl's hair." But you don't do it.	As the class leaves the room to go to recess, you take something off the teacher's desk.	You need to ask mom a question and you say, "I'm sorry for interrupting but..."	You ask to see a friend's toy and they tell you no.
A friend asks to play with your toys and you tell them no.	You don't know the answer on a test so you look at another student's paper.	The girl sitting next to you asks you for an answer on a test and you show her your paper even though you know you shouldn't.	You go into your brother's room and take some money on his bedside table.
You broke a vase in the living room while playing around and go tell mom you did it and apologize to her.	You apologize to a friend for not wanting to steal something for them.	You tell mom the reason you are late getting home is because there were 50 dogs chasing you.	You tell your dad you can't take out the trash because it's too heavy.

Using Music to Reinforce DBT Skills at Home

Homework is an essential component to learning. Providing these strategies in the classroom is step one, repetition is the next step. Teachers and therapists are encouraged to send these skills home through inviting the students to practice skills learned in class and the songs/activities with their family.

We believe that what the family/parents do, children will also do, and vice versa. So we recommend that parents/caregivers learn these skills for themselves and teach children through example and enthusiasm.

This book provides links to videos and recordings (see the Appendix for a full list and for a QR code to scan), so that families, teachers, adults, and group leaders have quick and efficient ways to learn new skills. The recordings and songs recommended are kid friendly and beneficial to the whole family. The resources offered are quick and efficient. For example, parents can create playlists to play at home or in the car on the way to school to help reinforce and practice the skills.

Posting reminders of the skills in the classroom will help the children use them consistently in the classroom, and we also encourage the students to have reminders at home. For example, post a STOP sign or pictures that signify rainbow breathing. We also recommend skill handouts for the family and reminders on teacher websites about the skills with the songs/activities included in this text.

The most powerful tool to strengthen skills at home is to ask your student to share the skills! Encourage them to sing, chant, play instruments, and do so mindfully. Pay attention to your child as they share. Encourage them to voice their emotions, to work through challenges, and ask for what they need.

Conclusion

Education opens the academic and emotional pathways in a child's life. Leading the way as a teacher, parent, caregiver, and/or therapist is rewarding and challenging, a dialectic in itself. This book has offered teachers and those guiding our children new and engaging ways to reach young minds through music. The included lesson plans are easy to follow and aim to support students' social-emotional growth by laying a foundation in DBT skills.

Our hope is that you and your children will use the dialectics, mindfulness, distress tolerance, emotion regulation, and interpersonal effectiveness skills in this book to enhance their lives. We also hope that you find that the benefit of using music makes the skills more memorable and applicable. The activities shared will reap rewards of skill development and generalization starting young and growing within the hearts and minds of those you touch.

Music helps us grow, learn, pay attention, feel, experience, interact, grieve, celebrate, encourage, live! Keep using music in your life to expand upon these lessons and skills, allowing creativity and growth to blossom in those you teach!

Appendix

Recordings of the following songs are available to view at https://www. youtube.com/playlist?list=PL0jguhoPs0m6qrlhhTR7P4PPtz7wuicy1 or by scanning the QR code below:

1. Mindfully Here and Now (this song is a variation of "All I have to do is breathe" by Patina Jackson. Find the original song on Spotify or Apple Music)
2. Notice My Breath (public domain)
3. Rainbow (original song)
4. Use my Senses (public domain)
5. Row, Row, Fact or Foe (public domain)
6. The Roller Coaster Ride (original song)
7. Worry thoughts, go away (public domain)
8. Pros and Cons song (original song)
9. Pros and Cons chant in the round
10. This is Just a Thought (public domain)
11. DEAR MAN (original song)
12. Fast Friends (original song)
13. Listening, listening; show interest in what you say (public domain)

References

CASEL (2023). *SEL Policy at the State Level—CASEL.* https://casel.org/systemic-implementation/sel-policy-at-the-state-level/2024

Chong, H. J., Kim, H. J., & Kim, B. (2024). Scoping review on the use of music for emotion regulation. *Behavioral Sciences, 14*(9), 793–793. https://doi.org/10.3390/bs14090793

Hwang, M. H. (2021). Interactive perspectives on mindfulness, music and music therapy: A literature review. *Approaches: An Interdisciplinary Journal of Music Therapy, 15*(1). https://doi.org/10.56883/aijmt.2023.90

Jones, S. E., Ethier, K. A., Hertz, M., DeGue, S., Le, V. D., Thornton, J., Lim, C., Dittus, P. J., & Geda, S. (2022). Mental health, suicidality, and connectedness among high school students during the COVID-19 pandemic—Adolescent Behaviors and Experiences Survey, United States, January–June 2021. *MMWR Supplements, 71*(3). https://doi.org/10.15585/mmwr.su7103a3

Klodnick, V. V., Kissane, B., Johnson, R. P., Malina, C., Ewing, A., & Fagan, M. A. (2020). Adapting dialectical behavior therapy for young adults diagnosed with serious mental health conditions in residential care: A feasibility study. *Residential Treatment for Children & Youth, 38*(3), 1–20. https://doi.org/10.1080/0886571x.2020.1751017

Lebrun-Harris, L. A., Ghandour, R. M., Kogan, M. D., & Warren, M. D. (2022). Five-year trends in US children's health and well-being, 2016–2020. *JAMA Pediatrics, 176*(7), 1–11. https://doi.org/10.1001/jamapediatrics.2022.0056

Leeb, R. T., Bitsko, R. H., Radhakrishnan, L., Martinez, P., Njai, R., & Holland, K. M. (2020). Mental health-related Emergency Department visits among children aged <18 years during the COVID-19 pandemic—United States, January 1–October 17, 2020. *MMWR. Morbidity and Mortality Weekly Report, 69*(45), 1675–1680. https://doi.org/10.15585/mmwr.mm6945a3

Linehan, M. (2015). *DBT Skills Training Manual* (2nd ed.). New York: The Guilford Press.

Mazza, J. J., Dexter-Mazza, E. T., Miller, A. L., Rathus, J. H., & Murphy, H. E. (2016). *DBT Skills in Schools: Skills Training for Emotional Problem Solving for Adolescents (DBT STEPS-A).* New York: The Guilford Press.

McCauley, E., Berk, M. S., Adrian, M., Asarnow, J. R., *et al.* (2018). Efficacy of dialectical behavioral therapy for adolescents at high risk for suicide: A randomized clinical trial. *JAMA Psychiatry, 75*(8), 777–788.

McCredie, M. N., Quinn, C. A., & Covington, M. (2017). Dialectical behavior therapy in adolescent residential treatment: Outcomes and effectiveness. *Residential Treatment for Children & Youth, 34*(2), 84–106. https://doi.org/10.1080/0886571x.2016.1271291

Mehlum, L., Tørmoen, A. J., Ramberg, M., Haga, E., *et al.* (2014). Dialectical behavior therapy for adolescents with repeated suicidal and self-harming behavior: A randomized trial. *Journal of the American Academy of Child & Adolescent Psychiatry*, *53*(10), 1082–1091. https://doi.org/10.1016/j.jaac.2014.07.003

Miller, A. L., Rathus, J. H., & Linehan, M. (2006). *Dialectical Behavior Therapy with Suicidal Adolescents*. New York: The Guilford Press.

Moore, K. S. (2013). A systematic review on the neural effects of music on emotion regulation: Implications for music therapy practice. *Journal of Music Therapy*, *50*(3), 198–242. https://doi.org/10.1093/jmt/50.3.198

National Association of School Psychologists. (2019). *Shortage of School Psychologists*. National Association of School Psychologists (NASP). https://www.nasponline.org/research-and-policy/policy-priorities/critical-policy-issues/shortage-of-school-psychologists

National Association of School Psychologists. (2024). State Shortages Data Dashboard (NASP). www.nasponline.org/about-school-psychology/state-shortages-data-dashboard

National Center for Education Statistics. (2022). More than 80 percent of U.S. public schools report pandemic has negatively impacted student behavior and socio-emotional development [Press release]. https://nces.ed.gov/whatsnew/press_releases/07_06_2022.asp

Perepletchikova, F., Nathanson, D., Axelrod, S. R., Merrill, C., *et al.* (2017). Randomized clinical trial of dialectical behavior therapy for preadolescent children with disruptive mood dysregulation disorder: Feasibility and outcomes. *Journal of the American Academy of Child & Adolescent Psychiatry*, *56*(10), 832–840. https://doi.org/10.1016/j.jaac.2017.07.789

Rathus, J. H., & Miller, A. L. (2014). *DBT® Skills Manual for Adolescents*. New York: The Guilford Press.

Sena Moore, K., & Hanson-Abromeit, D. (2015). Theory-guided Therapeutic Function of Music to facilitate emotion regulation development in preschool-aged children. *Frontiers in Human Neuroscience*, *9*(572). https://doi.org/10.3389/fnhum.2015.00572

Spiegel, D., Makary, S., & Bonavitacola, L. (2020). *Creative DBT Activities Using Music*. London: Jessica Kingsley Publishers.

Zapolski, T., Whitener, M., Khazvand, S., Crichlow, Q., *et al.* (2021). Implementation of a brief dialectical behavioral therapy (DBT) skills group in high schools for at-risk youth: Protocol for a mixed-methods study (Preprint). *JMIR Research Protocols*, *11*(5). https://doi.org/10.2196/32490

For further resources from the authors visit dbtmusic.com.

Jessica Kingsley
Publishers

JKP is a leading specialist global publisher at the forefront of social change. We aim to promote positive change in society and encourage social justice by making information and knowledge available in an accessible way.

Our specialist areas span autism and neurodiversity, health, social care, mental health, education, disability, gender, sexuality and complementary health and bodywork.

We're committed to publishing books that promote diversity and inclusion, including representation of diverse race and heritage, disability, neurodiversity, gender, sexual orientation, age, socio-economic status, religion and culture.

If you have an idea which you think would fit JKP's publishing, you can tell us about it directly by completing a proposal form at

www.jkp.com